MW01258863

To: Dione, God bless!
Ronnie Welch
9/17/2018

BURNING BUSH
BOOKS

SERMONS IN NUTSHELLS

DR. RONNIE WILLIAMS

BURNING BUSH
BOOKS

BURNING BUSH
BOOKS

Sermons in Nutshells

By Ronnie Williams

Published by Burning Bush Books

Copyright @ 2018 by Ronnie Williams

All rights reserved

No part of this publication may be reproduced, stored in any retrieval system, or be transmitted in any form, or by any means, mechanical, electronic, photocopying or otherwise without the prior written consent of the publisher, except as provided by United States of America copyright law.

First edition March 2018

For information about bulk purchases, please contact Ronnie Williams at ronniegbc@aol.com.

Manufactured in the United States of America

ISBN: 978-0-9997694-2-3

All Scripture quotations, unless otherwise noted, taken from the Holy Bible, New King James Version.

Cover Design: Ronnie Williams and Adrienne Mayfield

Visit the author's website drronniewilliams.org

Dedication

This book is dedicated to the memory of my father, Squire Williams, Jr., (June 26, 1926- Oct. 14, 2014). He was the smartest man I ever met. He only had a sixth-grade education. He used to say, "The truth doesn't care who tells it." I have found that to be a fact in my life. There are examples of truth everywhere: in nature, politics, personal problems, and observations. I am a student of truth and I have compiled many truths that God has given me over the years for this collection of mini-sermons.

During my morning meditations, God has given me some observations about life that will inspire, uplift, and even convict people to transform their behavior. Since truth cannot be patented, these pages contain material that teachers of the Word, preachers of the gospel, and Christians will find beneficial to their ministries. It is my prayer that these truths will provide inspiration to face the uncertainties of life.

I sincerely hope that these "Sermons in Nutshells" will bless your life and your ministry. While I advocate expository preaching, the observations are accompanied by scripture, but not anchored in the text which follows each entry. I am delighted that you have taken time to enjoy these divinely inspired nuggets.

Ronnie Williams, BA. M.Div., D. Min.

Generostee Baptist Church Pastor

Starr, South Carolina

Table of Contents

Acceptance

At the end of the day, it doesn't matter what they say or think, what matters is what you say and think. We must be comfortable with the person in the mirror, rather than the person who critiques us. Haters will hate; talkers will talk; but only you know the truth. Make it a resolution to befriend the person in the mirror by keeping it real with God and treat haters and talkers like landscape. Psalms 18:3

Adulation

The cheering and "Amen" you hear in the background is not always because you're so good, it might be audience empathy. Many musicians have walked away from the piano stool; many pastors have left churches; and even employees have walked away from their jobs because they over-estimated their worth. Don't be deceived by crowd response. Just because they are egging you on with shouts of adulation doesn't mean that you are indispensable. Sometimes it's because they want you to sit down. God has someone who can do what you do better than you—someone who will be in your position before the undertaker gets your body. Don't let people swell your head. They will say "Hosanna" one day and "Crucify Him'" a few days later. James 4:10

It's trite but true. If someone likes you, you can do no wrong. If they don't, you can do nothing right. Your critics aren't critiquing your work. They just don't like you and they use what you've done as an excuse to say it. If people don't like you, stop trying to win their approval. "If people hate you without a cause, it's impossible to give them a reason to like you." ~Emanuel Scott. Obey God, love people and ignore critics; you'll have a lot less stress in your life. Matthew 12

Anger

A bulldog can whip a skunk any day of the week, but he must first ask himself a question—Is it worth the fight? Let's avoid debating and arguing with people who are self-centered and attitudinal and focus our attention on people who are hurting and hungry for comfort. 2 Timothy 2:23

When someone blows up at you, most often, it was not because of the last thing you were arguing about. It is usually an accumulation of issues. The fuse was lit sometime in the distant past and it kept building until the explosion with the last argument. If we don't deal with petty things as they arise—disagreements, bruised egos, misunderstandings, they will smolder and burn. The next thing you know, someone will put you on blast leaving you like a deer in headlights asking, "What happened?" Let us run a virus scan on our hearts to make sure we're not harboring grudges with someone before we make a complete fool of ourselves. Get that thing settled today because tomorrow . . . BOOM! Matthew 5:22-24

He who angers you controls you. When we say, "I lost it" and gave him a piece of my mind, we actually did. If you think about how you've been treated long enough, eventually you will act on it. You have to stop thinking about it. Stay focused. Don't be someone else's dummy who is remotely controlled. Getting even never works. "Stand still and see the salvation of the Lord." Exodus 14:13

Apology

Apologize. You have nothing to lose and everything to gain. Even if you were not the one who was wrong; you are totally innocent; they started it; they deserve to be punished; or they are implacable, obnoxious, odious, and mean, apologize anyway. The best way to get even is to take away the energy of the argument. Do jujitsu on them; apologize and be the victor. Besides, you will feel a whole lot better because your spirit will be free to worship and praise the Lord again. Matthew 5:25

You can't trample over another person's feelings, pretend that nothing has happened, and expect God to bless you. Over time, the pain you've caused will fester and erupt into resentment. We are all imperfect humans, and we will occasionally offend each other, but God has given us a protective shield, it's called an apology. Go quickly to the person you've offended and watch the blessings of God shower down on you, if for nothing else but the freedom to enter into God's presence with gladness. Matthew 5:22, 23

Appearance

I called a dude "honey" the other day! He was at the cash register at Burger King in Atlanta. He had jewels in his ear, eyeliner on his eyes, dreads, and a high-pitched voice. I didn't know that he was a guy until the manager smiled behind him when I said it; I was so embarrassed. The moral of this story is: Be careful when using pet titles for people you don't know. Life is complicated nowadays; you have to be circumspect in everything you do. Ephesians 5:15

I walked up to the QT counter and there was a young lady dressed to leave very little to the imagination. A young man behind her said some inappropriate things to her and she responded by saying some nasty things to him. I thought of a saying old people used to say, "Stale bread always attracts flies." Now, I know the young man was wrong, but he just did what came natural for him. Ladies, if you don't want flies swarming around, take the bread off the counter.
1 Peter 3:15

We all have some physical flaws that we want to disguise. None of us looks like our profile picture. We work hard on our outward appearance, but only God can see who we really are. Wouldn't the world be a better place if all of us worked on the inner person more than the outer? Ephesians 3:16-19

Appetite

"Life is not just what we want; life is what we want most. Sometimes we have to give up what we want to get what we want most." ~Dr. A. L. Patterson. Our appetite for things must be brought under control or we will self-destruct. Just because there are 15 items on the menu doesn't mean we need to order all of them. Our lives depend on how we order from life's menu. Don't let your appetite be your god. Philippians 3:19

Attitudes

Have you ever noticed that you can tell when someone is smiling even on the phone? Our voice changes when we smile, not only our voice but also our attitude. Try it time next you get a phone call. Start smiling before you answer and the person on the other end will start smiling also. The most powerful tool we have as believers is encouragement. Spread a little cheer today. Smile, even on the phone. It will make someone's day. Hebrews 10:24-25

It's one thing to be broke, but it's something else to be satisfied with being poor. It's one thing to be ignorant, but it's something else to be satisfied not knowing. It's one thing to be unemployed, but it's something entirely different to be satisfied with being lazy. Your today will be your tomorrow if your attitude towards today stays the same. Just like a baby will cry if her diaper is not changed. Change your thinking and your future will follow. Proverbs 23:7

"Raise your words not your voice; it is the rain that grows flowers not thunder." ~ Rumi. Our attitudes play a major role in how we are received by others. It is not always what you say but how you say it. We communicate with our spirit; this is why sometimes people understand what we are feeling even if we don't speak. Check your attitude before speaking by thinking first. It is much wiser to choose what you say than to say what you choose. Colossians 4:6

Some things we will never see because our hearts are darkened. We may have 20/20 vision physically but be totally blind spiritually. God only reveals His secrets to people with a pure heart. Never argue with anyone who says, "I can't see that; it makes no sense to me." They are not deceiving you; they can't see it because it has been hidden from them. A pure heart has nothing to do with being sinless; rather it's about being open to the voice of the Holy Spirit. When we develop the attitude that God is always right, and we are always wrong, God will open deeper truths that will amaze us. 1 Corinthians 2:14

Authority

God has set some people over us and some people under us. In order to maintain authority over those who are under us, we must stay under the authority of those over us. I see a lot of "ministries" sprouting up everywhere and that's great if God has ordained it, but if these churches are being birthed out of rebellion against a godly pastor, all is for nothing. God never blesses rebels. You must be willing to submit to authority to qualify as a leader. 1 Corinthians 11:3

Ask questions—a lot of question—and then wait for answers. Question authority, the police, parents, and teachers—that's what they are paid for—politicians, spouses, children, and preachers too. Never follow anyone blindly. Don't be afraid to ask questions. No one can complete an assignment without proper directions, and no one can put the puzzle without all the pieces, so ask questions. Anyone who gets frustrated by questions may be hiding something, so ask questions. Matthew 7:7, 8

A part of the conversation about police killing our youth that needs to be added is the issue of some dad's failure to teach their sons to respect authority. There are rogue cops out there looking for a reason to shoot their gun, and there are young "gangster rap" boys out there who are flexing already over inflated egos. This is a combination for disaster. Dad, teach your son to respect all cops, especially the bad ones, and they may get a chance to come home. The Bible teaches that the last days will be filled with lawlessness—this is not just the populace, but also the police. Obey the law as closely as possible if it doesn't infringe on your beliefs; this is what pleases God. Matthew 24:4-13

Pastors, let's do some teaching about the biblical perspective of submission to authority. In virtually every case of Black men being killed by police, the victim was challenging the authority of the officer. As preachers we need to do some preventative maintenance and teach our flock to do exactly what the cops tell them to do. If we know our children are running loose in the jungle with the lions and tigers, would it make more sense to wait until they are attacked and then blame the animals? Or is it better to instruct the children how to survive in the jungle? Let's add the biblical mandate on compliance to authority along with sounding the alarm against injustice to our preaching and teaching curriculum. Titus 3:1

The worst thing a human can do to another human is to take advantage while the person is looking up to you. God did not create us with the same mental capacity. Believe it or not, you are smarter than a lot of people you come in contact with every day. It's the lowest form of humanity to abuse the trust of others for your personal aggrandizement. Preachers who know the Bible but use it to further advance their pockets, parents who abuse their children, men who use women for sex, women who use men for money will all give account to God. We should all live as if we are on camera because we are; God is watching. Revelations 1:14

6

I pulled up to a Church and was about to park in what I thought was a good spot until the parking attendant told me, "You can't park there!" I said, "I am the guest speaker." He replied, "Sorry, but that's not your spot." He followed by giving me directions about where to park. I obeyed him. When I finished my sermon, I said, "Everyone please stand." I noticed that the parking attendant was standing in the back of the church. He followed my instructions. That's the way authority is supposed to work. He had authority in the parking lot, and I had authority in the Church. Until young people learn this, we will have complete mayhem in our community. None of us are our own boss; we must listen to those who are in charge. 1 Timothy 5:17

Bible

No one is above a thought. No matter how consecrated, sanctified, and Holy Ghost filled we are, bad thoughts will come to us from out of the blue. Even though I am a preacher of the gospel, you would not believe some of the thoughts that have gone through my mind. Still, just because you had the thought doesn't mean you have to own it. The mind is the battle ground for sin and many of us are being held hostage and even defeated by the enemy who infiltrates our thoughts. Guard your mind with the Word of God. That's what Jesus did in the Wilderness of Temptation. If we don't know the Word, we will be defeated. Make a resolution to study the Word. Matthew 4, Luke 4

The Word of God will comfort the disturbed and disturb the comfortable. It will either draw you or drive you. God has charged men and women to declare His Word with power and simplicity. Many of us will give an account to God for catering to the masses by slinging ear candy. We have Christians today who have spiritual diabetes because all they get is the dessert rather than the meat and vegetables. The real truth doesn't always make you shout or say "Amen," sometimes it will make you say, "Ouch." Do we really love the truth? Hebrews 4:12

Updates! Don't you get tired of updates on your phone, computer, apps, and automobile. It wouldn't be so bad if when you updated the thing; it would be simpler. However, it becomes more complicated and you have to re-learn the entire process. Some people are suggesting that the Bible needs to be updated to be more inclusive and reader-friendly. Even though it was written hundreds of years ago, it is still relevant. Read the Word. Hebrews 4:12

The Bible is not a book of answers; it's a book of promises. If you're reading the Bible to get answers to why your child died, why you suffer with a life-threating disease or why hurricanes, tornadoes, and earthquakes ravaged your city, you won't find them. Suffering is a result of sin and some things will never make sense. Why do sinners prosper and saints struggle? Only God knows. We should never look for answers but latch onto promises; the greatest one is "I'm with you always, even to the end of the world." Matthew 28:20

All prophecy confirms the Word. If "the prophet" calls you to the front of the church and embarrasses you before the congregation, God is not speaking. The purpose of all prophecy is to build up the church not confuse it. Don't be duped because the prophet knows your name and address; remember you filled out a visitor's card at the front door. Let's study the Bible and stop depending on histrionics and sensationalism in church services. Any jaw dropping church service that glorifies man is not of God; the devil can work miracles too. 1 Corinthians 14:3

"Daniel was not in the lion's den; the lions were in Daniel's den" ~Dr. William Augustus Jones. The safest place to be is in the will of God, even if it means death. We marveled over the death of the twenty- one Coptic Christians who died at the hands of Isis, but this is simple fulfillment of prophecy. Don't be disillusioned by these events. Instead, rejoice at the accuracy of the words of Jesus. If Matthew 24:9 is true, then they shall deliver you up to be afflicted and shall kill you, and ye shall be hated of all nations for my name's sake" was accurately predicted. We can rest assured that Matthew 24:30 is also true: "And then shall appear the sign of the Son of man in heaven and then shall all the tribes of the earth mourn, and they shall see the Son of man coming in the clouds of heaven with power and great glory." Come Lord Jesus!

WWJD (What would Jesus do?) Remember this from a few years ago? Well, there's one better—WDTBS (What does the Bible say?) None of us really knows what Jesus would do. We can only guess and speculate about it. We wouldn't have turned water into wine, walked on water, put mud in a blind man's eyes, or been born in a manger, but we can read the Bible and it will tell us exactly what to do because it contains the mind of God. You don't have to run to your pastor's study every Sunday morning and try to get him/her to validate what you want and are going to do anyway. Read the Bible; it has all the answers to questions that God wants you to know. 2 Timothy 2:15

The Bible does answer some of our questions, but it is not a book of answers. It is a book about the Answer. Many preachers enter the pulpit on Sunday to address questions that people in our congregation have about life. We twist the text to suit our whims in hopes of dealing with the proposed problem. This is the wrong approach to preaching. Some of our questions will never be answered until we see Jesus, until then we must simply trust him. That is what every biblical text teaches, trust Jesus. If your sermon doesn't present Christ as the Answer who must be trusted, it wasn't the Gospel. 1 Corinthians 13:12

It is impossible to discover, attain or learn truth— it must be revealed. Because of our sinful nature, we are blinded from seeing hidden realties about life. Therefore, a PhD can read the Bible from Genesis to Revelation and come away with nothing but words, but an illiterate farmer can listen to his pastor and be filled with wisdom. Knowing truth has nothing to do with the head and everything to do

9

with the heart. God only gives truth to those with humble hearts. 2 Timothy 3:7

California Psychics? I was watching the BET Awards and saw a repetitive commercial sponsored by this group. I wondered what God had to say about them. Here's what I found. "Let the idols approach and tell us what will happen. The prior things—what are they? Announce them, and we'll think about them and know their significance. Or proclaim to us what is to come! Report things that will happen in the future, then we'll know that you are gods. Do good! Or do badly! Then we will all be afraid and fearful. Look! You are nobody, and your deeds are nothing. Whoever chooses you is disgusting." Isaiah 41:22-24

Many Christians are saying, "The Lord spoke to me and said . . ." While personal revelations may still occur, they are always inextricably tied to the Word of God. So, it is far better to say, "I read in the Bible where God said..." because every voice we hear is not necessarily God's voice. Test the voice that's speaking to you by the Word of God. 1 John 4:1

Beware of what's coming next when someone says, "My Bible says . . ." This phrase implies religious arrogance, spiritual dogmatism, and frankly it displays biblical illiteracy. A better choice of words is "The Bible says . . ." There is only one Bible and we should be dreadfully afraid to write our own. All of us should carry the same Bible, and all of them say the same thing. It's okay if we interpret passages differently, but it's still from the same Book. We need to eliminate the phrases "my Bible, my church, my message" from our vocabulary. Was it your cross that saved you? Mark 13:31

Who remembers all of the "prophecies" that go forth at the beginning of every year about this being the year of prosperity, peace, and plenty? One "prophet" used the numbers 2000, 10, and 7 to prove that 2017 would be a year of breakthrough. But where was the breakthrough? Where was the peace and harmony? Where was the plenty that was predicted by the contemporary seers? Every day we wake up to the same thing---hatred, violence, and upheaval. It pays to stick to the Bible— it's never wrong. 2 Timothy 3:1-3

A person who looks up to God never looks down on people. If we keep our eyes intensely focused on the Lord, we won't see race, class, bank accounts, or physical appearance. The Bible says we all came from the dust of the ground. ~Genesis 2:7. Dust on a lamp shade, a table top, a window sill or the ground is still dust. One hundred years from today, we all will have returned to where we came from—dust. The only time we should put our nose in the air is when we are looking up to God. Isaiah 6:1-8

Change

Jesus is old school but he's doing a new thing. Isaiah 43:19

God changed the name of Abram to Abraham, Jacob to Israel, Sarai to Sarah, Simon to Peter, Saul became Paul. Each time a name was changed it was because God was transforming that person into a usable agent for His Kingdom. God never leaves us like He finds us. He immediately starts to work on us by altering circumstances in our lives, especially for those of us who are not participating in His plan. Sometimes He has to cripple us to crown us, break us to bless us, and tear us to transform us. Why not yield to the hand of God and stop fighting Him? Start acting like what God wants you to become and save yourself a lot of trouble. Phillipians.1:6

The world is changing so rapidly and the Church needs to keep up. We can't afford to do 8-track ministry in a CD community. What used to work in reaching people, especially youth, won't necessarily work today. There has to be some balance in our approach by using Biblical methods and relevant programs/services. Our music, preaching/teaching and ministries can't remain the same if we hope to transform our neighborhoods. Let's face it. If your baptismal pool has not been filled in a year, you need to examine your approach-- something is wrong. The only thing constant is change. 1 Corinthians 9:20

There are three kinds of people in this world: those who make things happen, those who watch things happen and those who don't know/care what's happening. If you want something different, you must do something different. Doing the same thing reaps the same result. Explore, try and you will eventually succeed. You have been created to make changes and to do that you have to experiment. You'll never know if it will work unless you try it. Give it a go and stop procrastinating. Get you a promise from God and trust it—it works. Genesis 15

It is okay to question authority. If they are right, relent. If they are wrong, question them. Have you ever been riding in a car with a six-year-old? He will ask ten questions a mile and many times you will have to answer, "I don't know." This is by divine design. Young people are naturally gifted to be inquisitive. They won't accept "business as usual" or "just because" for an answer. As we age, we deplore change, and anything different from what we are accustomed to has to go. If you don't believe this, go to a church meeting. Ninety percent of the over 50 crowd will say no to everything. Let's embrace change; if it's for the better. God is old school but, He's doing a new thing. Isaiah 43:18-21

Learning to drive a car with manual transmission is difficult when you first start driving, but over time you will shift gears without thinking about it. This is because your mind establishes a pattern of thinking after repetitive behavior. All habits start with one act, and then eventually, those habits will determine your destiny. If you change your thinking, you will change your destiny. It's impossible to raise your standard of living without first changing the way you think. Guard your thoughts and change your destiny. Proverbs 23:7

If you are the smartest person in the room, leave the room and find one where your thinking is challenged. We only improve if we are pushed by challenges. If it's easy to do, it's not worth doing. Proverbs 27:17

When I was a younger pastor, I had an older member storm into my office and say, "If our forefathers could see what you're doing to this church, they'd turn over in their graves!" I thought to myself, "If they could turn over, they'd get up." She said this because she objected to the changes I was making. We must learn that change is not bad if it's anchored in Scripture. What worked "back yonder" won't work forever. We will become stagnant and ineffective if we don't observe the times. This is according to the only one who ever turned over in His grave, Jesus! Matthew 28:18-20

When was the last time you did something for the first time? If you can't remember, you will probably be in the same place you are in next year this time. God has placed a sense of adventure in us and He expects us to use it. He is the Creator. We are made in His image, so we should be creative. Change your routine, break some habits, and throw yourself recklessly into His promises. Stand on them. Hebrews 11:6

Let's refuse the fatalistic view that nothing will ever change. What if Medgar Evers had accepted that view? What about Martin

Luther King or the Freedom Riders? What if Jesus had believed that people will never change, where would we be today? The next time someone tells you that he will not vote in the next election, that he is finished trying to make a difference in life, or he has given up their child because it's useless, share your testimony. Remind him that tomorrow is coming whether he participates or not, but it will be a lot better if everyone does his or her part to make it better. 2 Corinthians 5:17

Many of us are living just for now, but tomorrow will bring a new now. The now of today will become the then of tomorrow, and the new now will become the then of the next day. Let's face it, times, people and things are continuously changing, and if we are to be relevant in the future, we must prepare by adjusting to the changing times. Even the Church cannot afford to become stale, stagnant and stuck in our vain traditions in times like these. God is old school, but He's doing a new thing. The future is coming. Let's get ready for it by broadening our minds to new ideas, concepts and techniques to face the challenges ahead. Isaiah 43:19

The scenery never changes when we travel the same route, and many of us know the landscape so well that we never look out the window. Stop complaining and do something about your view. If your life is not what you want it to be, make a conscious decision to change streets. Nothing changes until something actually does. If you don't change your ways, don't complain about the trip. Genesis 35:1-3

Do something different today. Take a different route to work, try a dish you've never eaten or engage a person that you've never talked to. Attempt to make a new friend. Life becomes boring when we live in a box, so get out of the box. Don't just think out of the box: get out of the box and live. "If you keep doing what you've been doing, you'll keep getting what you've been getting." Variety is the spice of life.

Therefore, God has given us a vast world full of challenges and exciting opportunities. Enjoy life. Ecclesiastes 8:15

God knows that comfort is the number one enemy to change. As long as we are comfortable in our situation, we will never willingly change it. When a baby needs a change, she cries because she's uncomfortable. It is the same with believers. Many reading this post can testify that we changed our lives not because we saw the light but because we felt the heat. The discomfort you are feeling today just may be the best thing that ever happened to you because God is challenging you. There is never progress without change. Deuteronomy 32:10-12

Character

Hardship reveals and builds character rather than distorts it. If people loot in a blackout, it is because the opportunity exposed who they really were. It wasn't the blackout that caused the looting; it was poor character. If you were hurt by someone, maybe it was because you misjudged their character. They were never your friend. They just waited for the right moment to inflict pain in your life. Stop brooding over what someone did to you and praise God that He allowed the hardship to come, so that you could purge your life of fake friends. Proverbs 17:17

Christians

Being average places us in an impenetrable comfort zone. No one who is average ever made a significant difference in this world or the church, not one. To do exploits as Christians, we must be more than just average, we have to be normal. The description of a normal Christian is seen in the Bible, and the description of an average Christian is seen on the streets. Why don't we see miracles, multitudes coming to Christ, and the destruction of evil today? It's because of average Christians. Remember, we can't run with the crowd and be seated in the victor's seat.

Isaiah 40:31

We should never let anyone define us but ourselves. When we accept labels, we accept limitations and compartmentalization. No one label can define us. We are multi-functional, purposefully diversified and divinely given many assignments. The only one who knows our purpose and destiny is God. He who defines us can predict and control us. The only label we should accept is "Christian." Let's wear that label proudly. Acts 11:26

Most of us grew up without health insurance, yet somehow those old remedies mama gave us worked. If we tried to use her "cures" today, we would probably keel over. It was not her medical prowess that helped us; it was God. God has a way of making up for our insufficiency and lack, and in spite of what we don't have/know, it works to our advantage. We did not have Obama care, we had "Your mama care" and God. Every child in America should have health care, but in spite of those who call themselves Christians in Washington who are fighting against this legislation, God will provide for His people. Exodus 15:26

I was watching a game where the New England Patriots were humiliated by the Kansas City Chiefs. What caught my attention was how Coach Bill Belichick handled the post-game interview. When he was asked about Tom Brady's performance, he said, "We'" have to pass the football better. When he was asked about running the football, he said, "We" have to run better. He even said, "We" have to do better coaching. What if the Church did this when one of us failed in life, got sick, or brought shame on the Kingdom? If NFL, NBA and MLB coaches have recognized the importance of a team family, shouldn't the Church? When one of us suffers, even if they are not in our local assembly, all of us suffer. When a Christian falls, the world does not point at the individual, they criticize the Church. We are the Body of Christ and we should live and die for each other. 1 Corinthians 6:17

Nothing satisfies the devil more than a disgruntled and disgusted Christian. Hold your head up today, regardless of your circumstances. If you are a believer, you're already a winner. The Gregorian calendar imitated the appellation for Leap Year, but the Bible declares that every day is a "Leap Day." Luke 6:23. Listen, the joy of the Lord is your strength. You have God above you, Christ for you, and the Holy Spirit in you, so why be sad? Look to the hills from whence comes your help; it comes from the Lord. Isaiah 35:6

We must stop trying to "one up" each other spiritually. God is neither impressed with our holiness/righteousness nor is He in awe of our ministries, so why are we trying to out-shine each other and shroud ourselves with titles, esoteric church regalia, and denominational aloofness? You can be a saint in shorts as well as a cleric's robe. God wants spiritual fruit, not religious nuts. ~Author Unknown. Be who you are; never pretend because God knows every heart. Psalms 139:23-24

"And you are supposed to be a Christian!" When you hear these words, rest assured someone is trying to manipulate you into doing something they want you to do. Some folks will attempt to use your testimony against you. They may try to exploit you for their advantage by trying to get you to co-sign a loan, lend money, or do them a favor. Christians are crutches, not bed pans. Nowhere does the Bible tell the believer to lie down like a door map and let the world walk over you. Be available to help, not to be used. Proverbs 20:4

Some of us look like what we've been through because we've allowed every attack, false accusation, and onslaught of the enemy to intimidate us. Welcome to planet Earth, where critics, haters and cynics work around the clock to discourage us from fulfilling our purpose. To survive with our mental equilibrium, we must develop the hide of a rhino, the feathers of a duck, and the shell of a turtle. All believers will make it to their destiny, but all of us will not enjoy the trip if we don't resist some company along the way. Choose wisely the people you let into your circle. Amos 3:3

Just having pity on someone and doing nothing to help is like wetting in a dark suit; there's a warm feeling, but no one notices. The difference between compassion and pity is that compassion has on work clothes. The Lord often places us in position to lend a helping hand so that we can represent Him by sharing the gospel. We are not just to give a hand out, but a hand up. Look for opportunities to tell others about Christ by relieving their suffering. James 2:14-17

Never gloat at anyone's downfall. God's chastening hand is terrible, but He does it because He loves us. Pray for fallen believers when it's their turn to be corrected; it may be yours next time. Hebrews 12:5-7

When are we going to stop judging people by the car they drive, where they shop for their clothes, and what they do for a living? If we determine success by material possessions we have a worldly view of life rather than a biblical one. According to the Scriptures, success is determined by how many people we've served not how many people who've served us. ~Matthew 20:26. The word Christian means follower of Christ. If we live up to our name, we should value what He values and walk as He walks. "Foxes have holes and birds have nests, but the Son of Man hath no place to lay his head." Matthew 8:20

Committed Christians see immigration as an opportunity to witness for Christ rather than an influx of low-life criminals and moochers. The Church must arm herself with creative approaches and programs that are geared to winning immigrants whether they are from South America, Asia, Europe, or Africa. Look at it like this—it saves us a trip to foreign countries that may place us in imminent dangers seen and unseen. Sure, substance is important, but let's be more concerned about souls. Matthew 28:18-20

Misery: Trying to hold on to something God has already released. Everyone that a Christian meets in life is intentional, but not everyone we meet is supposed to be permanent. Think about it— Joshua and Moses, Elijah and Elisha, Paul and Barnabas were all partners, but they all had to separate for the good of the Kingdom. To go higher on a ladder, one must let go of the lower rung and reach up for the next. Anyone God has released from your life has been replaced by a greater blessing, but we'll never get it until we release the old one. Acts 15:39

Someone, please explain to me how a Christian could not want all people to have health insurance. Please give me one scripture to support the view that only people of means should have the best health care. I'm serious, give me just one verse. Proverbs 14:21

"We have to learn to live more simply so that others can simply live." ~Dr. Emanuel Scott. Which is easier, saying that people are just lazy and don't want to do any better or making personal sacrifices to help the less privileged among us? The former, of course. As Christians, we are duty bound to not turn away from poor people by making excuses as to why we shouldn't help them. Excuses fool no one but the people who make them. They are thin-skinned falsehoods stretched tightly over a bald-faced lie. Proverbs 14:31

Is there anybody out there who remembers Herman Munster? Herman didn't know that he was ugly. When people ran from him out of fear, he wondered what was wrong with them. Don't get upset when people reject your beliefs, values and lifestyle. There's nothing wrong with you; it's their perception of you. We are beautiful to God, but repulsive to the world because we're different. Love yourself for who you are and stop trying to fit in. 1 Peter 2:9

Your mirror is your best friend; go take a long look at it. A man walking down the street looked through a window and thought to himself, "That is the ugliest man I've ever seen in my life!" Then he discovered it wasn't a window, but a mirror. The only difference between you and the culprit is that the culprit got caught. The church would be a much better place if Christians were more introspective and less critical of others. 1 Timothy 1:5

Be big enough to admit and admire the abilities of people who are better at doing something than you. There's no room for jealousy in the Kingdom. When one of us succeeds, all of us succeed. Nothing destroys ministry faster than jealous Christians. Instead of letting their light shine, some people spend their time trying to put out the light of others. Be an encourager. Learn to promote, push and prompt others to do their best, and God will bless you. Love looks through a telescope; jealousy looks through a microscope. James 3:13-16

Some Christians are doing more harm to the Kingdom than good without even realizing it. Being dogmatic, hard-nosed and ethno-centric does not make you a strong Christian. If people on your job hate to see you coming because they know you are going to try to "ram" Jesus down their throats, you should re-examine your witnessing approach. Foolish zeal belongs to immature believers who haven't learned to follow the guidance of the Holy Spirit. Let's remember that we represent Christ in the world and nowhere did He force himself on anyone. Proverbs 11:30

"When a man is getting better, he understands more and more clearly the evil that is still left in him. When a man is getting worse, he understands his own badness less and less." ~C.S. Lewis. A Church sign read: "This is a segregated Church – For sinners only. ALL ARE WELCOME." If everyone reading this message would take a long look in the mirror, the world would immediately become a much better place to live. The mirror does two things—it shows who you are now, and it also shows where you've been. Identifying the sins of others won't help us. Let's look at ourselves. A Christian should be as horrified by his own sins as he is his neighbor's. Psalm 51:4

Reminder: Christians are not perfect. We struggle with alcoholism, depression, sexual identity, drug addiction, divorce issues, racism, and evil thoughts just like everyone else. The devil wants the world to believe that we are perfect and we play into his narrative when we portray ourselves as icons of perfection. The only difference between a Christian and a sinner is the struggle. Christ has saved us from our sins, but we still wrestle with our sins. That's the only difference. If you are a Christian battling sin, rest assured, you will ultimately be victorious if you keep fighting. The Cross of Calvary guarantees you victory. Romans 7

Christmas

Nowhere does the Bible command us to celebrate the birth of Jesus. It does command us to celebrate His death, burial and resurrection each Sunday. But come to think of it, it never commands us to celebrate our own birthday either. But how would you feel if people you loved didn't show up at your birthday party? Pretty bad huh? Why then are so many churches closing their doors when Christmas falls on the 25th of December? Psalm 100

Many of us looked for gifts under the tree on Christmas morning but the gift was on the tree. The real Christmas tree was erected over 2000 years ago at Calvary. Our sins, sufferings, shame, and sicknesses were vicariously taken and our salvation was gloriously given on that tree. Have a wonderful Christmas with your families and friends. 1 Peter 2:24

Let's face it. We often judge people by how they look, what they have, and their athletic/artistic skills. This superficial evaluation of people often causes us to overlook many who would bless our lives. God often sends to us what we need in some strange packages. That's what Christmas is about. What the world needed came in a manger from the womb of a virgin wrapped in rags. The next time you snob somebody, just remember that person may be just the one you need to bless you. 1 Corinthians 1:27-31

Choices

Because you were born in a log cabin doesn't mean you can't move into the White House. Because you were born in slavery doesn't mean you can't establish an Underground Railroad. Because you were born the son of a Baptist minister doesn't mean you can't become one of the greatest civil rights leaders of all time. Just because you are a mere community organizer doesn't mean you can't become president. The fact is that your destiny is in your hands and materializes by the decisions you make. Regardless of your state or condition today, you can change it by making good choices and the first choice should be Jesus. Only He can turn your life around. Joshua 24:14-16

Most of us are where we are today in life because of some misplaced yes's and no's in our past. If we could go back and switch a few around, many of us would be a lot closer to our goals and a lot happier. It is not luck, chance, or fate that determines destiny, but decisions. Therefore, every choice we make should be undergirded with prayer. God has a purpose for us all and only He knows the future. Church, it's praying time. Luke 18

If you have to go to Kay Jewelers to get a kiss from your sweetheart, you have the wrong sweetheart. Christmas is so commercialized that the real meaning has been lost. Let's refuse to stress if we don't have the money to buy gifts and simply send a message of "I love you" even if we have to personally write it. For those who truly love us, it would mean a lot more. 1 Corinthians 13

Church

A radical world needs a radical church; a radical church has radical ministries, and radical ministries are implemented by radical leadership. Rather than standing around echoing our culture, we've got to go militant on Satan's kingdom. He has stepped up his game, and he's taking the gloves off. Let's follow suit. No more business as usual. Let's vow to be radical in our witness, our worship and our praise. It's the right thing to do because we serve a radical God. Joshua 1:3:7, 8

Let's not get excited when someone from across town joins our church. Usually, we are just absorbing some other church's problem while doing no damage to Satan's kingdom. There is no advantage for God's Kingdom when we swap members and call it "church growth." Growing the church means winning the unchurched in the streets, out of the clubs, bar rooms, and drug houses. There is a difference between growing and swelling--growth is permanent. Swelling is temporary. Witness to someone today! Proverbs 11:30

"I can have church at home; I can watch church service on television; I don't like crowds; I can have church by myself, and I have to work on Sundays." Haven't we all heard these excuses for not attending church? Some of us have even used them, but did you know that it is a sin not to go to Church? We are commanded by Scripture to congregate and fellowship because we represent the Body of Christ. Every Christian should be a part of a local assembly and should attend regularly because it is a place to tithe, a place to go for spiritual support in crisis, a place to share your spiritual gift(s), and an example to the world of the Body of Christ. Go to Church on Sunday. Hebrews 10:25

The best investment a church can make is in its pastor. Churches will spend millions on programs, real estate, and campus equipment, but pay their pastors peanuts. If you prayerfully select the right pastor, the financial part will take care of itself. It's amazing how a charlatan can accumulate a cult following that doesn't question where the money goes in a ministry, but gospel preachers are literally starved by their congregations. If a deacon is reading this—pay your pastor, so he won't have to moon light to feed his family. Don't let a cult following treat "Slick Willy" better than you treat a Man of God. 1 Timothy 5:17, 18

Someone has said, "You can always tell how good a restaurant's food is by how many cars are in the parking lot." We've all heard this statement and to some degree it's true, but not so with churches. While on vacation, I stopped by a small country church and sat in the back. There was no Hammond organ, large choir, or skilled musicians. The preacher wasn't seminary trained and didn't command the pulpit, but the presence of God was in that place so strongly that I cried almost all through the service. God spoke to me and said, "Many are looking for the crowd, instead of Me." Go to church this Sunday to experience Jesus not the crowd. Matthew 18:20

A Christian who says "I love the Lord, but I don't like Church" is like a man telling a woman, "You have a pretty face." What about the rest of her (body)? Christ is the head of his Church and it is an insult to Him to declare love for Him and reject his body. If you truly love the Lord, you will love his body also. Find a church and be faithful to it, and your love for Christ will flourish. Colossians 1:18

In spite of the hypocrites, non-righteous politics, mishandling of money, and rude personalities, Jesus went to church. Maybe He is telling us something about the importance of worship. What's your excuse, again, for not being in church on Sundays? Luke 4:16

One of two things is happening. Either the people you hang with are becoming more like you or you are becoming more like them. We should not be reclusive from the world, but we need strength to be effective. Therefore, church fellowship is essential for strong witnessing. It is impossible to be a soul winner without having faithful church attendance. 1 Corinthians 15:33

The megachurch is great. God is growing His people, but don't be ashamed because your church is small. Remember, God rarely used a crowd. He often picked a handful, so that He would get more glory. We need both megachurch and small churches to complete His Kingdom. Be proud of your church wherever you worship. I love the Church. Matthew 16:19

Jesus did not tell the church to clone itself; He said to make disciples of men. He gave these instructions because we are all different and will respond differently to the gospel. Still, we should ultimately be loyal to him. What many of us call evangelism is nothing but an attempt to control the lives of others. Let's stop trying to make mini-me's and let people be who they are so they can win the people God has given them. No church is the only church from which people can go to heaven. Matthew 28:18-20

Many of us fault some police departments for racial profiling, and rightly so, but is the church guilty of doing something very similar? Are you a member of a church because of how your pastor and his wife look? Or the image they portray? Remember that it's often not what it seems. How do you respond when someone comes to your church tatted up or laden with piercings? What is your attitude towards someone whose sexual orientation is different than yours? What about a person whose race is different than yours? In many instances we've failed some glorious opportunities to share Christ because we judge by appearance. Let' stop profiling visitors who come to our church and be consistent with the gospel we preach. James 2:1-4

Some people go to church to learn how they can make things better for themselves. Others go to church to learn how they can make themselves better. The reason so many people leave church services unfulfilled and disillusioned is because God is not concerned about making things better. His objective is to make people better. When people become better, things will become better. Think of how much better your home, community, and this country would be if all people were good. Let's work on ourselves, and our surroundings will change. Romans 8:28

"If you want to go fast; go alone. If you want to go far, go together." ~Cory Booker. God has knitted us together so that we can conquer and overcome the world. Some Christians are not "active" in church and have a "take it or leave it'" attitude, but to be an obedient Christian, one must regularly attend church. If we only considered FB posts, it would seem that everyone is a Christian, but how many of us actually go to church? Find a house of worship and attend it faithfully. Colossians 2:2

It's not hard to determine when to pack it in and call it quits—check the fruit basket. When the season is over, the fruit ceases. Anything that lives will produce after its kind, but when it dies, it becomes fruitless. Life is too short to attend a dead church with a dry pastor where no one ever gets saved. Life is too short to continue in a relationship that causes pain to both parties. If you keep doing what you've been doing, you are going to keep getting what you've been getting, Change your position. Psalms 1:3

The church is not a showroom; it's a maintenance shop. It's not a haven for saints but a hospital for sinners. Therefore, no Christian can afford not to be a member of a church. We are all works in progress and need the spiritual support that is only found in a Bible believing, teaching and obeying church. It's one thing to talk Christianity on

Facebook, but it's another to be an active member of the church. Find a church home. Hebrews 10:25

"When one of my members tells me that the Lord told them to leave the church, I say that's good because I learned not to argue with God." ~Dr. Tony Parks, President of SCCCE. Jesus told under shepherds to go retrieve lost sheep not disgruntled ones. Pastors, let's stop wasting our time baby-sitting rebellious people who want to take their ball and bat and go home when they can't get their way. More often than not, when someone leaves your ministry it's because God is really speaking to them or the devil. In either case, it is a blessing to the sheep you have left. 1 John 2:19

Church behavior and language have changed since I was saved in 1976. Back then, we didn't high five or turn to your neighbor nor did we find three people to share our testimony with. These changes may be necessary to keep church services exciting and relevant to millennials, but there are two words that should never have dropped from the Church's vocabulary--Amen and Hallelujah. Amen means, "I'm in agreement." Hallelujah means, "Praise the Lord." Together they mean, "I'm in agreement with praising the Lord." Now, that's Church in a nutshell. Revelation 19:4

The Church is in dire need of discernment. We mistake emotionalism for the voice of God. We misconstrue gifts/talents as the anointing and equate the success of a person as God's approval on their life. As a result, the lifestyle of a person doesn't matter to us anymore, but rather how they are received by the public. The public is not an acceptable measuring stick because the majority of the public hates God. If you want to know if something is of God, read the Bible. God has said nothing else since the last verse in the book of Revelation. Revelation 22:19

I saw a guy on the track walking around with running shoes, a sports outfit, and ball cap, but he was smoking a cigarette. I don't know what his physical goals or ambitions are, but obviously they are not very high. Some people go to church in the same fashion. They look churchy and participate in the service like everyone else, but they have no expectations or goals. All believers worship with expectations and objectives; otherwise, their worship is in vain. Psalm 138

We go to the dentist to get help with our teeth, and we go to the doctor to get help with our bodies, but before going to the dentist, we brush thoroughly, and before going to the doctor we take a bath and put on clean underwear. There are women who will fix their hair before going to the salon because they don't want the stylist to chide them. Aren't you glad we don't have to fix up before coming to God? The church ought to be the only place where people can come just like they are without being berated or belittled. Let's be that church. Revelations 22:17

The Church is doing more damage to evangelism than drug dealers, prostitutes and gambling casinos combined. The world sees us as a bunch of self-righteous, money hungry hypocrites. Our insensitivity to the plight of poor children while we proclaim our advocacy for the unborn, our abhorrence of foreigners in the U.S. while sending missionaries overseas, and our open support for amoral political leaders whose only concern is another dollar all give credence to their claims. Here's a suggestion to the Church: let's try loving people, regardless of nationality, creed or color as did our Lord. Let's spend more time preaching at gas stations, Wal-Mart, and grocery stores than we do under the bright lights of the pulpit. When the world sees that we care about them, the elect will come to Christ and be saved. Titus 3:4

It's amazing to hear the anti-emotional comments about an enthusiastic church service coming from Christians. What's wrong with being emotional? God created us to be emotional, and it should play a part in every church. It has been said that enthusiasm is nothing but faith with a tin can tied to its tail. Some of the same critics of an emotional service will scream until they are hoarse at a sports event but choose to sit placidly serene in church. He who has no fire in himself can't warm anyone else. It's the enthusiastic worker who gets promoted, and the enthusiastic teacher who has the best class, it is also the enthusiastic church that wins souls. A cold church is like butter; it doesn't spread well. Psalm 100

I bit my tongue while eating and it hurt so bad that I stumped my feet— yes both of them. My teeth and tongue disagreed momentarily, and my whole body suffered. Both my teeth and my tongue were doing exactly what they were designed to do, but they were not in harmony. When we get out of place in the body of Christ, the entire body suffers. If you don't have the gift to sing, don't join the choir. If you don't have the gift of hospitality, you shouldn't be an usher. If God didn't call you to preach, please stay away from the pulpit. Don't make the church suffer. "When people go to sleep in church, somebody should wake up the preacher." ~Author Unknown. 1 Corinthians 12

"I love my church" is a wonderful sentiment, but "I love thy kingdom" is much better. The word kingdom is used 369 times in the Bible (215 Old Testament and 154 New Testament) and the word church is used 111 times. It is only in the New Testament that Jesus taught more on his kingdom than he did his church. It's great to love your church, but we should love all people, even those who don't come to our church. When a Baptist or a Methodist suffers, Presbyterians and Lutherans should feel the same pain. Be careful about being exclusive: you might shut out Christ. We may have a different banner over our door, but we have the same cross on our steeple. Matthew 6:10

Think of your left foot. Before you read the first sentence you were not thinking of your left foot at all, unless it was in terrible pain. Likewise, all the members of your body can only be felt when you think about them. You brain constantly monitors your body to make you aware of problems with it. When something is wrong with any part of your body, your head takes command over every part to go to the assistance of the ailing member. It tells your feet to go to the medicine cabinet. It tells your hands to grab an aspirin, and it tells your mouth to open and your throat to swallow— all to aid the ailing member. Don't you wish the church would operate in the same fashion? 1 Corinthians 12

Are we promoting our church or Christ? We all love our church, but do we all love the Lord? Some of us are treating our church like a pyramid scheme. We solicit new members by telling them all the good things that our Church is doing, how good our pastor preaches, and what benefits are available to members. Remember Jesus didn't send His disciples to preach the church but to preach in His name. Learn the difference between being a church salesman and a disciple. Be a soul-winner not a church recruiter. Acts 5:42

Think about it. Everything you've eaten that has given you nutritional support was once alive. Anything you consume that has never had life in it does your body no good unless it is medicine. Medicine actually only challenges your body to heal itself. The medicine doesn't heal you; it is your body's reaction to it. In the natural something had to die for you to live, doesn't it make perfect sense that the same is true in the spirit world also? Jesus lived. No historian will deny this fact. He died, which is also a recorded historical fact. He is also alive and well and lives in His body, the Church. Praise God for life through His Son. Revelation 1:18

Every day, wear the face that will be on your obituary. There are happier faces on bottles of poison than on some Christians. If every person in every church could be his pastor just once and see the faces he has to look at on Sunday mornings, they would be surprised. When visitors come to our churches and see us looking like we've been baptized in lemon juice, they can't wait for the benediction. It is the joy that's in our hearts that draws people to Christ, not our spiritual depth. Nehemiah 8:9-12

What if everyone in the world were exactly like you? What if all of the voices in the choir sounded alike, and all instruments only had one cord and played in one key? What if all preachers delivered their sermons just alike? What if everyone in the church looked, dressed, behaved, and talked the same as you? Then nothing about you would be special. Why, then, do we attempt to make others in our own image, and criticize them for doing and saying things we disagree with? No two people on the planet are alike. This is by divine design because God enjoys diversity. Quit trying to clone yourself and let others be unique. Happiness will follow when we resign from being CEO of the universe. Let people be themselves. "No one can whistle a symphony, it takes an orchestra." ~Unknown. 1 Corinthians 12

What if the church were more like the local bar? They have happy hour (church service) at the bar and people are waiting at the door to get in (punctuality). Liquor and beer are dispensed liberally (grace). No one in the bar judges the person next to him (forgiveness) and people are not shocked by anything they hear (brotherly love). They are liberal in buying each other drinks (sharing). Secrets are shared openly and no one repeats it the next day (unity) probably because they don't remember. Everybody there is looking for relief from pressures of the world (acceptance). We can learn a lot from heathens. This is the test of true Christian ministry. The ebb and flow of the church is to do whatever it takes to get unbelievers to come. But when they come, what do you have? Making compromises with the world will never grow a strong church; it will only swell with worldly people. Stick to the truth of God's Word. You can't go wrong with that. It will be the last thing standing when all of fish sandwich seekers are gone. John 6:25-27

Compassion

Until you have driven up to the driveway of your church on Sunday morning, and broken down in tears, you haven't done much pastoring. When as pastor, you see the devastation, disease, immaturity, divorce, drug addiction, rebellion, spiritual apathy, financial stress, foreclosure, and bankruptcy that affect the people you are leading, and it should have an effect on you. Preachers, all we have is the truth. Tell it. That's the only thing that will set people free. God help us not to give out ear candy on Sunday just for an audible response or applause. The church hurts and all real pastors hurt along with her. Watch and pray for your congregation. 1 Samuel 12:23

Doesn't it annoy you when people evaluate your situation by using theirs as a model? Just because you pulled yourself up by your own boot straps doesn't mean that everyone else can. If you were blessed to achieve greatness, good for you, but others may not have the ability, stamina and resources you have. The Church has no place for narcissistic members whose testimonies center around I, me and my. We should never use our accomplishments as a paddle to spur others on. Whatever happened to compassion? Stop talking about yourself and listen to people. You just might learn something. Luke 10:25-37

Competition

The world tosses around the term "best"—who's the best quarterback in the NFL, the best player in the NBA, and the best R&B singer, but this word should never be used in the body of Christ. Commercialized and competitive Christianity will ultimately be judged and those who participate will lose their reward. God never asks us to be the best. He tells us to be faithful with what He has given us. As far as God is concerned, the usher is just as important as the bishop. Don't feel that your efforts are overlooked by God, they may be by men, but God sees everything you do for the kingdom. "Be thou faithful unto death." Revelation 2:10

What is it about a crowded church and a microphone that makes some people turn into Martin Luther King or Luther Vandross? If you're given two minutes to speak at a funeral, it's just rude to talk ten minutes and then sing. This isn't "Who's Got Talent." It shows insensitivity to the bereaved family to take advantage of their pain to "put on a show." Let's learn to do what we're asked in the time allotted and sit down. 1 Corinthians 13

No one church or denomination has exclusive rights to the kingdom of God. If you listen to some pastors, God has only given us the real message of truth and the only way you can get to heaven is to be a part of our church. Hey all, God isn't Baptist or Methodist or COGIC or Full Gospel or Pentecostal, nor is He in the Christian Center. He's God all by Himself and He speaks through more people than your pastor. We are like the carnal Corinthians arguing over who is the "best" preacher/singer. Let's take our eyes off people and put them on God. Acts 26:26

If I went to an R&B concert I'd expect Usher, Alicia Keys and Mary J Blige to croon, swagger and play to the crowd. That's what people pay them to do; therefore, it's in order for the show. When I go to church, I don't want to see a performance. What's wrong with singing and sitting down after you've finished? Real saints can see through histrionics for the sake of getting attention.

Let's not debate who the best preacher is, who has the best voice, who has the largest membership, whose budget is the largest. Why not leave this trivial stuff to the world to argue? It does not belong in the Church. We are the body of Christ that has been fitly joined together on earth to express His will. Every part of the body is important. If you don't believe that, stomp your little toe on the dresser in the middle of the night and watch your entire body writhe in pain. Mature Christians don't debate titles (apostle, prophet, bishop, reverend, arch bishop). Call a brother whatever he wants to be called and work with him/her for the kingdom. If we don't believe what we preach and teach, let's get out of the Church and show the world how to go to hell. If we do, let's love and respect each other. Mark 3:24

Complaining

I've had some good days. I've had some hills to climb. I've had some weary days and some lonely nights, but when I look around and think things over. All my good days out weigh my bad days. I won't complain. It's a great song but bad theology. Even if your bad days out weigh your good days, you still shouldn't complain. Complaining expresses distrust in God. Wherever you are in life, God led you there and He has a reason. Romans 8:14

Count your blessings not your troubles; count your friends not your enemies; count joys not your sorrows; count your healthy days not your sick ones; and count the teeth you have not the ones you had pulled. We spend too much time emphasizing what the devil has done to us rather than what God has done for us. My Dad used to say, "Don't worry about the mule going blind, just load the wagon and hold the line," God has promised to take care of His own. Let's believe Him. Romans 8:31

Complaining never helps; it only alerts the enemy of his success. The only way the devil knows what's going on in your head is to hear it coming out of your mouth. Don't seal your destiny to failure with negative words. God created us for greatness. When we complain, we're essentially calling God a liar. Stop complaining. No one wants to hear it anyway. Trust God. He will work this thing out for your good. You can't see it, and you're not supposed to, but this too shall pass. 1 Corinthians 10:10

The greater the opposition, the greater the opportunities. No discovery, invention or legislation came into fruition in a vacuum. Each was met with opposition. If it's easy to do, it blesses no one. Expect haters to come out in full when you are advancing the cause of the kingdom and thank God for them. You need haters to push you to greatness. Stop complaining when people turn their heads when you drive up in a new car, sing in a church service, get that degree, get married, or buy a new home. Praise God because a blessing is behind it somewhere. Matthew 27:50

When someone complains, it's not the complaint that we should listen to, but the complainer. Usually, there's a lot more behind the complaint that doesn't meet the eye. Your spouse is not mad just because you squeezed the toothpaste at the top and not the bottom or that you left the toilet seat up or down. Many other things led to the explosion that you need to consider. So, rather than trying to fix what they are complaining about, get to the root of the problem by examining your relationship as a whole. Start by establishing clear, honest, and open communication. Proverbs 21:9

We have heard that the squeaky wheel gets the oil, but that's not what God says. God says that the squeaky wheel often gets replaced. Some people live to complain. They complain about the new church bus, the loudness of the organ and guitars, the length of the sermon, and where the money is being spent, but if you check the financial report, they are the ones who give the least in offerings. Always watch the complainers; according to them nobody can bless the church but them. Numbers 11:1

Why allow someone to live rent-free in your head when they don't care about you? Trying to get even, repeatedly voicing negativities about the hurt they caused you, or constantly predicting their doom only hurts you. Let it go! Get over it and move on with your life because you're wasting time singing that sad song about how bad they hurt you. Evict free loaders from your mind! Only rent to people who will take care of your property. 1 Peter 3:8-10

Confession

Why does God demand that we confess? Well, it's simple. When we confess, we acknowledge that we are sinners. The most miserable person in the world is the person who walks around pretending. It's better to be wrong and true to yourself than to be right and insincere. I would rather have a hater around me who's real than a friend who is phony. "Con" means "with" and "fess" means "to talk." When we confess, we talk with God. We admit what God already knows. Tell Him the truth about yourself. He's listening. James 5:16

Conscience

Some of us walk into a room and we think everyone is looking at us. We see people laughing and talking, and we feel like they are talking about us. Then we read a post on Facebook and think the post is about us. Have you ever thought for a moment that the conviction you feel is of the Holy Spirit? When you are convicted it may be that Holy Spirit is shining a light on your sins. God convicts us, but Satan condemns and accuses us before God the Father to show our unworthiness. Put your sins under the blood and stop being so jittery. 1 John 1:9

People don't snap; they drift. When you hear of heinous acts like the downing of the German Wings plane, the Columbine massacre, or the Boston bombing, rest assured that these atrocities were not the result of "being pushed over the edge." Little by little the human mind is corrupted by the kingdom of darkness until it explodes and self-destructs taking others with it. Guard your thoughts. Monitor what amuses you because it could be destroying your conscience. James 1:14

We raised pigs when I was a kid. My dad told me that once a pig got out of a pen, it would be hard to confine him from that point. This is true for any animal—horses, cows or even dogs are included. It is also true with our conscience. Once we have violated the parameters of established teachings and moral conditioning, it will be difficult to go back to the pen of morality. Protect your conscience; never go beyond the boundaries of scriptural admonitions. There is a severe price to pay when we venture out of our pen.

"Do what's right, not for others, but for yourself." ~Socrates. If you do wrong long enough, it will start to look like it's alright to do it, but there's no way to make the right thing the wrong thing to do. What happens is that your conscience becomes hardened and desensitized to the way it was nurtured. Many times, we ask how someone could do such a thing; it wasn't easy for them. They had to override their conscience many times before they got the nerve to do it. It pays to obey your conscience. Zechariah 7:11-13

Cooperation

The winning team and the losing team play with the same ball. The difference is that the winners manage the ball better. Two people can grow up in the same house and community with equal intelligence. One can end up enjoying life to the fullest while the other one ends up miserable. The difference between the two is how they manage circumstances. All of us will have setbacks, haters, and critics, but to overcome them we are going to need to have determination. A setback is simply a setup for a comeback. Let Jesus be your manager; it's a sure way to win. Hebrews 12:1, 2

I kicked over an ant mound. Immediately the ants collectively started rebuilding. Not one of them looked up to see who did it. They did not form a building committee to elect a chair person, vice chair, and secretary. Not one cared what color the other one was or whether they were male or female. They didn't seek legal advice to determine if whether I should be sued. There was no shouting, bickering or finger pointing about who was to do what. They all stayed in their lane. It didn't seem that any of them negotiated a salary contract to make sure they would be properly paid and insured. They just went to work, immediately, rebuilding what I destroyed. Maybe, ants need to be in charge. Proverbs 6:6-11

I just saw two Holstein bulls mashing heads together trying to establish their territories. I thought to myself, "If they had any sense they would put their heads together to figure out a way to get out of that pasture because tomorrow they both might be at the slaughter house." We are supposed to have dominion over cattle, but we behave like them when we fight over politics, positions, people, and possessions. Tomorrow may be our dying day, why not put our heads together to make a better tomorrow for our families and communities?

Crucifixion

God's greatest work is not the creation of the sun, moon and stars. Neither is it the formation of the ecosystems on planet Earth. The heavens declare the glory of God and the Earth shows His handiwork, but you don't look up or down to see God's greatest gift to mankind. To see God at His best, one has to look inward because His greatest work is the forgiveness of sin. God was at His best on Calvary. Today, you may be burdened with guilt and laden with regret because of something you've done, but you don't have to be. Simply ask God to forgive you and He will do it. Satan tempts us to sin then accuses us afterwards to make us feel miserable. Turn the table on him. Go down on your knees and tell God. He loves you and will forgive you. Psalms 130:4

It is impossible to crucify yourself. You may be able, with much determination, to nail your feet to the cross. It is feasible that you could use one hand to nail the other hand to the cross, but there's no way you can pin that last hand. To be crucified, there must be a second party involved who hates you enough to inflict excruciating pain on you, and who wants you to die. But unless you are crucified, there will be no resurrection of power. To have additional power in your life you must be crucified and then resurrected. Tell me again, why are you mad at your haters? Galatians 2:20

Dating

I am amazed at the number of Christian women who visit "dating sites." I always believed that whenever you order from a catalog, you never know what you're going to get until it shows up at your door. According to the Scriptures, the man is to be the pursuer. I've never gone fishing and had a fish jump into the boat and say, "You got me!" Sisters, if you BE the right woman, God will SEND you the right man. The best dating site for the believing woman is her prayer closet. Proverbs 18:22

Guys, you should always know who your daughter is dating, even if you're not with her mother. A boy needs the challenge of a man, so he will be accountable for what he does with and to a girl when they go out. A strong man needs to be standing in the doorway when they get back from the prom to greet both of them. I know times have changed, but some things never change. Boys will always respect another man. Both a man's daughter and the boy she dates will AWAYS remember the example you set as a father when they were dating and will appreciate it later in life. 2 Corinthians 11:1-3

A lot of societal pressure is placed on a young woman to get married just so she can say "I got a man." Here's a biblical rule to follow. Never date someone who doesn't share your values and beliefs because dating can lead to marriage. If you fall in love with someone you don't like, "till death do you part can be a long time." Make sure that the person you're dating shares your faith and is not just showing up at your church to get you. The Church has lost many young Christian young ladies "to wolves in sheep's clothing" who lured them away from the church by pretending to be saved just to get them. Once they got them, the mask came off and they resorted to their real selves. The only man you need, young sister, is Jesus. 2 Corinthians 6:14

Devil

Distractions are a part of the enemy's arsenal. He used them against Nehemiah, Peter on the sea of Galilee and even Jesus in the wilderness. You will be distracted today, but it's not the distraction that derails you; it is your reaction to the distraction. Keep your eyes on Jesus no matter what. You will make it. Hebrews 12:1

It's never as bad as it seems. If your spouse left you, you lost your job, you can't meet deadlines for bills, you are faced with sickness, you have to rear unruly and unsettled children, or are diagnosed with a terminal illness, you must remember one thing. All this is a form of demonic intimidation strategically designed by the enemy to discourage you. Remember, if God brought you through "that" which denotes distance, he can bring you through "this" which means the present. The devil wants to magnify our problems so that we focus on the "now" and lose sight of "then," but know this: God is more interested in your destiny. Trust Him. You're coming out better on the other end. Psalms 27

"It's not how long you live, but how well you live." ~Dr. Martin Luther King. The devil is not trying to destroy both the quality and quantity of your years. Living a long life of evil is a testimony of the power and influence of the devil; therefore, the longer one lives, the more glory Satan receives of that life. A short life lived helping others, loving God and exhibiting the fruit of the Spirit sends a greater message of God's power and glory. Manasseh lived 67 years, Josiah lived 39 years, but Josiah's leadership had a greater impact on history because he lived for the Lord. Let's pray for a good life rather than a long life. 2 Chronicles 33:1; 2 Chronicles 34:1

Life is too short to worry about what someone else thinks about us, especially when we know we've done the best we can. All God requires is that we put forth our best effort. He will take care of the rest. Then He gets the credit, and we give Him the praise. "If we please God, it doesn't matter who we displease. If we displease God, it doesn't matter who we please." ~Rev. Jasper Williams

The devil wants you to think you don't matter, you're not good enough, you're not smart enough, you're insignificant, and whatever you attempt to do will ultimately fail. Remember, it was one man who brought all of us into existence—Adam. One woman is the mother of all of us—Eve. One man saved humanity from extinction--Noah. It was one man who delivered Israel from Egypt—Moses. It was one man who died at Calvary for us all—Jesus. You may be one person, but you can make a world of difference. You matter. Vote. Jeremiah 29:11

According to Dictionary.com, the definition of opposite is "being the other of two related or corresponding things." When something is opposite of another, the two completely oppose each other in values, appearance and power. It follows that the devil is not the opposite of God because his power is not contradistinctive of God's power. The devil's power does not offset the power of God. The opposite of God is unbelief. The only thing that ties God's hands on your behalf is doubt and unbelief. If you can believe, you can have God's power right now at your disposal. Believe and you can receive. Matthew 19:26

Settling with our past accomplishments/achievements is the same as giving up. Life is painful. We hurt, and the tears are falling, but this is just another bump in the road. The devil would like nothing better than to see us lose heart and give in to discouragement. Just over the hill is a beautiful valley, but we must climb the hill to see it. Remember, God didn't create us just to survive. He created us to thrive. Don't quit! Stopping on third base is the same as striking out. Tell the devil to go to hell and keep going. Galatians 6:9

Discernment

One of the most important gifts today in the Kingdom is the gift of discernment. If you can't discern the difference between hurting and seeking people and spongers and freeloaders, you will become a victim rather than a witness. People are won when we follow the leading of the Holy Spirit. We are entry ways to the Kingdom not doormats. Don't let people use you because of their indolence. Be attentive to hunger for spirituality and not those who are driven by the monster of idleness. Proverbs 19:24

Let's not mistake pretention for piety, charisma for character, posturing for practice and sermonizing for saintliness. Learn to watch for what happens after the applause—when the lights are off and the cheering stops. God help us to see those in leadership positions in the Kingdom who have hidden agendas. No preacher is perfect, but all preachers should strive for perfection. Matthew 7:15

Divine Protection

I grew up riding a bike without a helmet, swimming in a pond without a lifeguard, riding in a car without a seatbelt, walking in the woods without snake-proof boots, taking castor oil for colds, climbing trees without a harness, wearing no shoes in the summer, drinking water out of a well, driving a school bus at 16, and had no healthcare. Someone asked me why I don't travel with armor bearers. I smiled and remembered that I do. They are called goodness and mercy. Can you relate? Psalm 91

Doubt

Unbelief is irrational. Don't buy the hype when someone tells you they are too intelligent to believe in God. It makes no sense. Common sense will tell you that God exists. Anyone who believes that all creation is an accident is not being rational; they are simply refusing to acknowledge the truth. Proof that God exists is in the mirror. Education should not be an excuse for atheism but a reason for faith. If someone has a degree, he ought to have enough sense to know that God is real. It's not that people can't believe; it's that they won't believe. God has mandated that everyone who comes to Him must believe. Do you believe? Psalms 14:1

Dreams

Want to know if someone likes you? Tell them your dream. It never fails. If they like you they will encourage and rejoice with you. If they don't, they will discourage you and give you fifty reasons why it won't work. This is also a barometer to determine if your dream is big enough. Let's stop playing it safe. Let's dream so big that the devil will tremble in his boots! Keep dreaming BIG things for God. Genesis 37:9-11

Pay close attention to your dreams. Sometimes God will speak to you in your sleep and warn you of pending danger of enemy attacks. Not all dreams are of God but don't discount them because often the only time we will listen is when we are asleep. Sometimes we have dreams because we eat too much and go to bed before the food digests. The difference is that when God is speaking, there is always a biblical precedent. Read the Word. We can rejoice because we are under 24-hour surveillance. The angels keep watch and they will give warning when the enemy approaches. Matthew 2:13

Encouragement

Have you ever noticed that Rolls Royce and Bentley don't run commercials? The value of their product brings their customers to them. When you know your value, you don't have to beg people to be your friend or your mate, to spend time with you, or to love you. Be confident in the fact that God made you just like He wanted you. Everybody can't afford or handle luxury.

Some people light up a room when they walk out. It's as if they have a dark cloud over their head all the time. Negativity begets negative results and positivity begets positive results. Let's spread cheer rather than gloom today and lift up someone's bowed down head. Proverbs 12:25

God summed up His creation with the announcement, "It is good." Everything He made is good. Alcohol is good. Have you had cold medicine lately? Marijuana is good. Ropes for ships are made with hemp. Sex is good within the context of marriage. Misuse of these things can be evil. Facebook is good if we don't misuse it. Let's use this medium to build, encourage, and spread cheer. Someone needs it today. 1 Thessalonians 5:11

In forty years of ministry, I have discovered that my best cheerleader is me. Sometimes you have to encourage yourself because if you wait for others to give you a "pick me up speech," you'll be waiting a long time. Some people say it's strange to talk to yourself. God says that sometimes it's necessary to have a conversation with your soul. Remind yourself who you are and who you belong to and watch the difference in your attitude towards others. The truth of the matter is, if you don't have joy, you will make a poor witness. Get alone for five minutes and remind yourself who you are and that moment will erupt into praise. Psalms 34:1-3

The best way to get even is to get better. If you were denied entrance to a college because of low grades, get a tutor, study harder and apply to a better school. If you were not hired because of your lack of experience, take a lesser job, get some training and find a better company. If a person leaves you for someone else, fix yourself up and the next time you see them, throw them a kiss and walk away smiling. Let's take every negative experience we endure and use it for motivation to get better. Philippians 1:12, 13

When you feel like giving up, go on. When you feel like they don't understand, stand. When it hurts so bad it seems unbearable, bear it. When you feel like you can't take it anymore, take it. As cheerleaders on the sideline cheering on their team, sometimes your spirit must do the same with your soul. Tell yourself that quitting is not an option; victory has already been accomplished. We simply have to have patience to wait and see the result. Stay strong. Psalms 34

Eliminate Stressors. Hebrews 12:1, 2

Stop wasting your time trying to figure out why people don't like you. That's a fruitless venture. Everyone is not supposed to like you. Some people are in your life to comfort you, while others are there to chase you to God. There are only two categories—comforters and chasers. Both of them are given by God to bless you. Isaiah 43:7

"God never opens Red Seas for us to go back into Egypt." ~ E.V. Hill. Keep moving forward. Don't look back, and God will work miracles on your behalf. Don't expect God's help if you turn back. God never blesses His displeasure; He only blesses that which brings Him glory. You may not be able to see it today, but there's a Canaan ahead. Exodus 14:15

You can't bury Christians; you plant them. They told you that you couldn't do it, you wouldn't make it, and you'll never get it, but look at what God did for you. If God did it for you the last time, He'll do it again. Being planted doesn't feel good. It's dark; it's cold; and it's painful, but that's necessary for you to sprout. Hang in there, you'll see sunshine shortly. 1 Corinthians 15:4

Don't get drawn into negative conversations with instigating people who don't like themselves. People attack others because they feel insufficient in their own lives. To make themselves feel better, they spew negative venom on anyone who is attempting to come up in life. Concentrate on improving your life and not going back and forth with little people who don't like themselves. Let's focus on the "mark for the prize" and not on the mess created by little people. Philippians 3:13, 14

No, that outfit will not look as good on you as it does on the mannequin. So, if that's your objective for buying it, save yourself some cash. Millions of dollars are spent on clothes by people who want to look like a dummy. It's impossible, but the good news is you can look like God made you. Be satisfied that God made you unique, distinct, and different from anyone else on the planet. You were fearfully and wonderfully made, so accept yourself as a divine master piece of art. "I am somebody cause God didn't make no junk." ~ Ethel Waters. Psalms 8

We usually compare greatness with the soaring of an eagle, but we forget that buzzards soar as well. Greatness has little to do with how high one flies; rather it is more about how you react when you fall down. Being great entails the mental fortitude of refusing to wallow, complain, and make excuses for falling, and getting back on your feet when everyone has counted you out. Flying is temporary: falling is inevitable. All of us will fall eventually, but the greatest of us will get back up. If you have fallen, the choice is yours, don't accept defeat. Get up. Mark 9:31

We only have two choices; we can kick someone in the pants or pat them on the back. Life gets hard at times and often it is not because of a lack of faith but because of faith. The number one tool of the enemy is discouragement which comes from people who don't even realize they are being used. Be conscientious of the words you use when engaging people. You never know who needs reassurance. Encouragement is like premium gasoline: it helps to take the knock out of living. Acts 20:1-2

You'll get a lot more out of people from a pat on the back, than you will from a kick in the pants. ~ Unknown. My car had a strange knock in the engine, so I asked the service manager at the dealership about it. He suggested that I use premium gasoline rather than regular. I followed his instructions, and just like that—no more knocking. Encouragement works the same way. It takes the knock out of life. Let's learn to stop always pointing out other's faults and applaud them for what they are doing right. God is not the only one who likes praise. Your spouse, your kids, and co-workers do too. Acts 20:2

Evangelism

Jesus did not tell his disciples to go into all the world and make mini-mes, he instructed them to make more disciples. The Church is spending too much energy attempting to force people in uniforms designed by creeds, catechisms, and denominational ideologies. We are to be in unison not uniformity. Unity comes from power (love) within. Uniformity comes from a power (pressure) on the outside. God never intended for all of us to be alike. There should be unity in diversity. As an old church mother used to say, "We have to catch a fish before we can clean it." 1 Corinthians 12

Example

We are addressing a culture today unlike any in history. Just about everyone you meet on the street has heard of Jesus because of modern technology (Internet, TV, printed page), but hearing doesn't mean sound waves permeating the outer ear causing a vibration on the ear drum which sends an audible signal via nerve endings to the brain. Hearing, as far as the Bible is concerned, means acknowledging the truth of the gospel. People have heard enough sermons. They need to see an example of the gospel lived out in our everyday lives by what we say, how we treat each other and how we love and live. Let's stop shouting from the soapbox and start living as Christians at home, on the job and in the streets. Philippians 3:17

Excuses

We will find a way to accomplish anything we are passionate about. Excuses are produced when we really don't want to do what's being asked of us. The next time we give an excuse, let's ask ourselves what the real motive is. Remember, with God's help "All things are possible." Philippians 4:13

Experience

"How can you tell me anything when you did the same thing?" We've heard this question coming from our youth and some of us have even asked others the same thing when they were trying to correct us. But come to think of it, who is better to give advice than someone who has experience. If I've been down a road and have seen that the bridge is out, I'd be less than a friend not to warn you of the pending danger! The pains we suffer qualify us to be experts in certain areas, so share your pains with others and warn them even if they don't want to hear it! God sends us through things so that we might bring others out. I am ashamed of many things in my past, but those are the things that I can speak with authority on because I've "been there done that." Hebrews 4:15

Facebook

Facebook is my shepherd. My spiritual growth shall want. It maketh me to sit down and do nothing for hours because it requireth all my leisure time. It keepeth me from doing my duty as a Christian because it presenteth so many good posts that I must see. It restoreth my knowledge of what trivial things my friends are doing and keepeth me from the study of God's Word. It leadeth me in the paths of failing relationships and being useless in the Kingdom of God. Yes, though I live to be a hundred, I shall keep checking my inbox as long as it will work, for it is my closest companion. Surely frustration and resentment shall follow me all the days of my life I will dwell among the misinformed forever. Amen.

If Jesus put up a post on Facebook, most of us would give it thumbs down, even though we pretend to pray to him for every prayer request we read. What if he posted this? "I want all who are reading this post to be born again (John.3:6) then find a Bible believing Church and attend regularly, (Hebrews 10:25), love ALL people unconditionally, (John.13:34, 35) pray for everyone who hates you (Matthew 5:44), abstain from worldliness (Titus 2:12), and last but not least, tithe of all your earnings (Malachi 3:10). One has to wonder how many likes He would get.

Faith

You can attempt to deny me health insurance and accuse me of driving up your insurance premiums. You can fight against affordable housing for me, and then accuse me of living in squalor. You can deny me a decent education, and then accuse me of being ignorant. You can discriminate against me by establishing systemic racist practices, and then accuse me of being lazy and non-productive. You can jail me disproportionately because of my race, and then accuse me of being prone to criminal behavior. But what you can't do is oppress me and accuse me of not having faith. God loves me in spite of how you treat me. Justice will prevail because He will have the last word.

Let's face it. We are not happy all the time. Sometimes we don't feel like smiling, saying nice things, being polite in morning traffic, being patient in line, saying forgive me, praising God, or praying. Hey all, it isn't about how we feel, it's about how we faith. We can't live by feelings because they change with the wind. We do what's right because of our faith. Romans 1:17

To a large degree, God allows us to set the limits of our own blessings. If you need a blessing, the Lord says, "According to your faith, be it unto you." If you don't believe God, you are actually saying that God can't be trusted, and if He can't be trusted, then He is a liar. If He's a liar, He's unholy, and if He's unholy, then He's unworthy of our worship. So, the key to your promotion is in your hands not God's. All things are possible to him that believes. Numbers 23:1

There is not a home in the world that can place a sign on the front lawn that reads "No Hurt Here." Every human has been emotionally damaged by someone/something which has caused blinding tears. The loss of a loved one, a bitter divorce, an unfaithful spouse/friend, imprisoned child, sickness, and pain are common to all. The good news is your tears will soon turn into triumph, your hurts to hallelujahs, and sorrows into joy, if you are saved. We have a rock-rib promise in God's Word that we can stand on. Listen, have faith in God. Time will eventually heal all wounds. God promised! Psalm 30:5 declares, "Weeping may endure for the night, but joy comes in the morning."

"And so it happened just as the Scriptures say: Abraham believed God, and God counted him as righteous because of his faith." Genesis

15:6. He was even called the friend of God. James 2:23 Notice the verse didn't say that God was a friend to Abraham, but rather that Abraham was a friend of God because there is a difference. To be a friend of God one must submit to God's rules, commandments, and ways. If God were our friend, He would have to submit to our demands, ways and desires. Listen, God is not our pal, buddy or side-kick, He's God. We must do as Abraham and believe and trust Him in everything. Only then can we become "a friend of God."

Stepping out in faith does not mean the abandonment of common sense. If you have Smart Car income you should not be driving an Escalade and using Philippians 4:19 as justification. Faith is reading His Word, interpreting it correctly, through the aid of the Holy Spirit, and acting on it. God gave us the ability to reason, and He expects us to use it. He wants us to plan and be good stewards over our gifts, money, and time. Let's learn to get a vision, make the necessary sacrifices for it today, plan our future, and trust God to fill in the blanks. Hebrews 11:8-10

Playing it safe inhibits greatness. To make a difference in this world, we must do something extraordinary which means we must take risks. No one gets the fruit from the tree without going out on a limb. Confound the nay-sayers, haters and experts; take a risk. The farmer will never reap a harvest unless he risks his seed. A father will never produce a strong family unless he risks his time. A Christian will never please God unless she risks her faith. Find a promise in the Word and take a leap of faith. Hebrews 11:6

As it is written, I have made thee a father of many nations, before him whom he believed, even God, who quickeneth the dead, and calleth those things which be not as though they were. Romans 4:17. This is probably the most misinterpreted verse in the book of Romans because many believe that it empowers them to speak anything they want into existence. Notice, however, that it speaks of God calling things which that are not as though they were. It is impossible for us to call anything into existence unless God orders it through us. We can only stand on the Word of God and wait until He brings it to pass. Like Abraham, let's find promises and stand on them.

Like money is the medium of exchange in our economy, faith is the medium of exchange in the Kingdom of God. Heaven's wealth (love, peace, joy, gentleness) is available to all who use faith in God's Word. You can have a pocket full of money and be as ragged as a potato vine if you don't spend that money. You can also have faith, but it is a dead faith, if you don't use it. Why not take a chance and simply believe the Word! If God said it, I believe it, and that settles it? The truth is if God said it, that settles it, whether you believe it or not. Why not believe it? Matthew 24:35

Calling that which is not as though it were is just lying. That's what a liar does. He says things that are not true. Just because he keeps saying untrue things will not make those things true. We can't speak anything into the atmosphere, call things into existence, or decree blessings on anyone. What we can do, like Abraham, is stand on the promises of God and not stagger or compromise. If God said it, speak it with confidence, declare it, decree it and then believe it. The power is in God's Word, not ours. Romans 4:17-25

Every human has faith. The person who sits down at a slot machine is exercising his or her faith. When we drive the interstate at 70 miles an hour, we have faith. The farmer who puts a seed in the ground has faith. When we go to the pharmacy, buy medicine we can't pronounce, from a person we don't know, with a prescription from a doctor we had to pay, we are practicing faith. But biblical faith only works when it is in God, and only grows when we hear the Word. ~Romans 10:17. Some people's faith is not strong enough to bring them to church services, but they expect it to take them to heaven. Go to church Sunday and get your faith lifted. James 2:17

The devil doesn't want your health, wealth, or your family. He wants your faith. If he can get your faith, he can have anything else you possess. You may be suffering with financial problems, disease and domestic issues, but as long as you have faith, what God has, you have also. Faith keeps the person who keeps the faith. No one lives in doubt who prays in faith. Hebrews 11:6

False Prophets

"Therefore, declares the Lord, I am against the prophets who steal from one another words supposedly from me. Yes, declares the Lord, I am against the prophets who wag their own tongues and yet declare, "The Lord declares." Indeed, I am against those who prophesy false dreams, declares the Lord. They tell them and lead my people astray with their reckless lies, yet I did not send or appoint them. They do not benefit these people in the least, declares the Lord." Jeremiah 23:30-32. The next decree, prophecy or Word you get from a prophet, ask him where it is in the Bible.

A dead giveaway of a false prophet/prophetess is the use of personal pronouns. Whenever you hear the continual use of the words, "I, me, and my," know this: God is not speaking. What a deceiver wants to do is to show himself as larger than life when all men/women are basically the same. We are all sinners. Listen carefully to the one who is giving you spiritual advice to see if God is talking or if the person has a personal agenda. If God is speaking, you can find confirmation in the Bible. "Thus saith the Lord." Isaiah 7:7

Family

Sometimes people who burn bridges can never go back home. Just as sure as you leave home, you're going to cross some bridges, and to get back home, you must cross those same ones coming back. If you set one or all of them on fire, your return trip is impossible. One place we all ought to be welcomed is home. It's there where you were nurtured, inculcated, and groomed to be whom you are today. Don't ever forget this one important fact. Everything back home may not have all been pleasant, but it was there that you were shaped for your future. Always remember those who contributed to your success. "The same people you meet on your way up the ladder, you will meet coming down." ~ Squire Williams

Take care of your aging family members; it's commanded in the scriptures. They took care of you, sacrificed for you, and nurtured you, when you didn't know your right hand from your left. Many of us have more than they ever dreamed of and we have what we have because they stood in the gap for us. Now that they're old and can't help themselves, how could we neglect them when they have nowhere else to turn? Shame on us if we forsake the people who made us who we are today. When you know you've done the best you can for them while they were living, you won't make a fool out of yourself at their funeral. 1 Peter 5:5

Parents discipline your children. It's not "cute" for a child to break into grown folk's conversations or walk between them while they are talking. If you let them tell you what they are going to do and dictate the agenda at home, they will go to school and attempt to do the same thing—giving an already frustrated teacher an additional headache! You can't wait until he/she is 16 to start disciplining them; it has to start in the cradle. If you don't chastise them now, they will chastise you tomorrow. Proverbs 22:6

So, you think cussing, disrespecting authority and twerking children are cute? Just wait a few years and then see how cute they are in prison, in teenage pregnancy or in the cemetery. The greatest investment a person can ever make is in their children; they are our future. The Bible has a repetitious phrase, "He served the God of his father." All children will follow the God/gods that their parents served. If you go to church, take your children. If you pray, let your children hear you. Read the Bible to your children; it sticks to their little minds! Do you want your child to serve the God/god you serve? Genesis 46:1

It takes more power not to do what you are able to do than to actually do it. Yes, God is able, but sometimes He refuses to do what we ask because He is a good Father who knows what's best for us. Just because a parent can, doesn't mean that they should give their children what they ask for. Use discretion in parenting. Let your children earn their own money to buy those sneakers. They will appreciate them a lot better when they have sacrificed to get them. They are not interested in old stories of how you had to work as a child; they can't relate to that. You have to show them. Giving children everything they ask for is not an indication of good parenting. Isaiah 42:14

When was the last time you saw kids outdoors playing? The internet and modern technology are great tools but they must be managed. A kid needs to play in the dirt, go fishing, walk in the woods, learn about animals and insects, plant a seed and watch it grow. These things alone will sharpen their faith in God. Only a fool can observe nature and doubt the existence of God. Tell your kid to go outside and play. Psalms 14:1

Should all kids get an award? Absolutely not. All kids should get a reward for their work, but not an award for just participating in a contest. A reward is given for a hard day's work; it's called a paycheck. An award is given for an exceptional performance in a required field. We contribute to our kids' egos and vanity when we hand them awards for mediocre efforts. Let's teach our children that nothing is given in this life; they must earn it. We do them a disservice by not teaching them the value of hard work. 2 Thessalonians 3:10

Take your children to the woods and let them see the trees, insects, and animals. Take them to the beach and let them get sand between their toes or make them go outside and get dirty. It won't hurt them, I promise. No rational thinking human can be exposed to nature and deny the existence of God. We've taught our kids what to think, not to think, and that inhibits creativity. Have you noticed that all music sounds the same and all cars look the same? There is a sameness that prevails in virtually every field of endeavor. That's because there's no creativity today. Teach children how to think, not what to think, and God will reveal himself to them. Psalms 19:1

When we see kids fighting at school, apartment complexes, and restaurants and posting the disgraceful melee on YouTube, we say, "How sad!" It is sad, but the problem is not delinquent kids. The real problem is delinquent parents. God never meant for children to raise themselves. When your kid reached for the cookie you told her not to touch and you thought it was cute when she went behind your back and took it anyway, you contributed to the problem. It may be too late to change some of the kids in these videos, but the ones on your lap need to be taught discipline. Parents, teach your kid to respect you first, then themselves, and they will respect authority. Proverbs 22:6

Accountability nurtures affection. Parents who demand accountability from their children know that their kids will appreciate them later in life. Husbands who are held accountable by their wives will love their wives more, and churches that hold members accountable will be loved more by their membership. Pastors, don't be afraid to insist on accountability from members, especially ministry leaders. If they hold a position of leadership, they must be accountable to you, as you are accountable to God. The reason people love their church is because their church holds them accountable. Hebrews 10:24, 25

Sometimes all your children need is your approval. We often downplay the achievements of our kids in an attempt to push them harder. What if that accomplishment was their best? Our children need our validation and when we don't give it, they will feel as if they are failures. Be positive with your children and tell them how much you appreciate their efforts. You will see the difference. Proverbs 16:24

We've got to determine whether we want to be liked or respected. It is possible to like some people without respecting them. On the other hand, there are some people we respect, but we don't like them. We may not like the police, but we must respect them. We may like our friends but make insulting jokes about them. Parents, God did not give you children so that you could make them like you. It's great if they do, but your main objective should be teaching them to respect you. If you're paying for groceries, clothes, shelter, and tuition, make sure you're respected. Your children may not like you now, but they will definitely appreciate you later in life. Leviticus 19:3

Mom, if you teach your children to disrespect their father because you despise him, eventually they will disrespect you. It may have been a bitter breakup/divorce, and he may have been the cause of it. He may also be a deadbeat dad who never helps with parental responsibilities, but you should maintain a measure of consistency and integrity and teach your children not to hate their father. Children understand a lot more than we think they do, and they will respect you when they are older for how you taught them to respect all people, even their dad who contributed nothing to their nurturing. It's a hard thing to do, but it will be worth in the end. 1 Peter 2:17

A comet lights up the sky and turns every head that sees it for three or five seconds, and then as fast as it appeared, it vanishes. The sun has been in the heavens for millions of years, but most of us never even look up in the morning. Isn't it strange that the people who are the most flamboyant, talented, and athletic get our attention so quickly, but the people who have undergirded us, supported us, and are there for us through hard times are often overlooked? Rihanna, Tom Brady, Leonardo DiCaprio, LeBron James, and others are lighting up the sky right now, but what about your spouse, your children, and your church fellowship? Pay more attention to people who actually know your name and who will be there for you when you need them. Proverbs 17:17

Most of us spend time planning for the future. Some of us spend time talking about what happened yesterday, but few of us are enjoying today. Plan for your future and learn from your past, but don't forget that today will never come again. Live as God would have you live. Take time today to talk to your kids/spouse, avoid the drive-thru, and sit down at the dinner table with your family. Enjoy today. Yesterday is gone, tomorrow might not come. We only have today. Psalms 118:24

One of the cruelest things a person can do is to use their children as weapons against an estranged spouse, grandparent, or other family members. Sure, you were hurt by them, but that doesn't give you the right to inculcate hatred into your kids. Hatred corrodes the container and is like a rifle with a plugged barrel. The backfire can be more destructive than the shot. If they are truly bad people and deserve your estrangement, let your kids find it out for themselves. They will appreciate you later in life. If your kids end up hating other family members, don't let it be because of you. Proverbs 10:12

Your family can get away from you and you may wonder, what happened? Your sons and your daughters might do some things that will make your jaw drop, and you simply can't believe that they are your kids, but if you have put the fear of God in them from birth, never worry. They may stray, like we all did, but they can't get away from the seed of God you've planted in them. Children brought up in Sunday school are seldom brought up in court. Proverbs 6:22

Be positive. Don't just tell kids what not to do, tell them what to do. "Stop running down the hallway." This statement is not as effective as, "Walk down the hallway." You accomplish your goal with both of these statements, but the latter tells the kid exactly what to do. Jesus took the Ten Commandments which included both "'shalts and shalt nots," and condensed them into one positive affirmation, "Thou shalt love the Lord thy God with all thy heart, and with all thy soul, and with all thy mind. Thou shalt love thy neighbor as thyself." Lesson: We are much more effective controlling human behavior when we think, act, and speak positively. Matthew 22:37-40

Blowing out someone else's candle will not make yours shine any brighter. Criticizing what people enjoy will never convert them to your way of thinking. Telling your teenager that rap music is horrible, her hair looks weird, or castigating your son for his drooping pants serves no purpose but to ostracize and isolate them from you. You can't make someone see what you see by lambasting them for something they like. Put your mind in reverse. Your parents hated the way you dressed, the music you enjoyed, and the way you did your hair, but you turned out just fine. Yes, monitor your kids' dress, habits and behavior, but be careful how you chastise them. The only way to correct bad behavior is by setting an example of better behavior. It is a great person who empathizes, a good person who sympathizes, and a small person who criticizes. Proverbs 16:20

If your child is rebellious, he/she doesn't need encouragement, they need a whipping. This sounds harsh, but it's Bible. Never encourage anyone who is wrong and rebellious: reprove him. Preachers, don't mount the pulpit every Sunday to "knock it out the park." The world is in disarray because preachers are not telling people the truth. The world hates the truth, so don't expect to get the "key to the city," look forward to being run out of the city. We must stop this charade of conforming to the world to win members. Preach! 2 Timothy 4:2

Faultfinding

You don't have to look hard to find fault in people, so why bother looking. Let's accept the fact that there are no perfect people and move on to something constructive like encouraging and influencing them to try harder to improve. Fault finders work shifts to prove the obvious, and when they discover your faults, they expose you so they can feel better about their own faults. Because there are no perfect people, there are no perfect homes. Since there are no perfect homes, there is no perfect church. If you find a perfect church, don't join it because you are going to mess it up. Stop looking for fault in others and concentrate on self. Luke 23:4

It doesn't matter what you do, how good you are, or what you attain, someone will always find fault in you while making excuses for himself. It should be everyone's resolve to never seek public approval for anything because it's impossible. As long as your heart is right with God and you're grounded in Scripture, ignore your critics and continue the course. 1 Samuel 12:24

People who have the most to repent of are the most judgmental. When you encounter a person who always finds fault, watch them carefully and keep your distance. They often want to get close to you so they can find a good place to stick their knife. They hate something about themselves, and it makes them feel better when they can find something wrong in others. Go to your cell phone and delete some contacts or change your number before that spirit becomes attached to you. Matthew 16:1-12

Don't criticize anyone if you don't have a better solution. You don't have to search hard and long to find fault in people, because we are all human and humans have foibles. If you want to find fault, go look in the mirror. Criticism without suggesting an alternative is just hating. Proverbs 12:15

Maligning you by pointing out your faults doesn't mean I'm telling the truth. When I hear arguments against the Church, most times they are directed to the foibles of a "crooked preacher." Granted, there are some crooked preachers, but what does that mean about your personal salvation? At the end of the day, every one of us must give an account to God for ourselves. Our argument to Him cannot be, "Lord there were crooked preachers in the church." There are crooked bankers, but you still put your money in the bank. There are crooked doctors, but you still go to the hospital. Don't lose your soul by watching the preacher. Revelations 20:11-15

Favoritism

The people we dismiss may be the ones we miss. The Chicago Bulls essentially dismissed Michael Jordan in 1998 and have not won a championship since. The Carolina Panthers dismissed Josh Norman and look what happened to them. Some people create chemistry just by being present, and no one can fake that. It's true that "one monkey don't stop a show," but the absence of one monkey can make the show a lot less interesting. Be careful who you overlook.

At some point we must stop assigning blame about who's at fault and go to work on the problem(s). Every day the headlines are filled with finger pointers and fault finders while our adversaries abroad are laughing with glee. We've gone from, "Speak softly and carry a big stick," to yelling and carrying a switch. God help us! If there ever was a time the church needed to pray, it's now. Let's pray for this country and our leaders, not their agenda, but that God's will be done. Pray. 1 Timothy 2:1-3

We don't have to look hard to see fault in each other because we are all human. Since this is a reality of life, why point a finger at anyone. The adage is true, when we point one finger at others, there are always three fingers pointing back at us. Remember, mud throwers never have clean hands. When we see the wrong in others, it doesn't make us better than them because we sin differently than they do. Spend more time looking in the mirror than looking through the window. Psalms 51

Fear

Farmers place scarecrows in their fields to scare crows away and it works. There's no danger involved in approaching a scarecrow. It can't harm the crows, but they don't know it. They're frightened away by the appearance. If crows had any sense, they would look for scarecrows because wherever there's a scarecrow, there's something good around. Whenever something frightens you, know that Satan is trying to keep you from something good that God has for you. Psalms 27

Flesh

Let me testify. I have all the trouble I want trying to control myself. I have no time to try to control someone else. Why don't you do yourself a favor and give up the attempt of dictating to others how you want them to live their lives. If you ever become CEO of the world, which will be never, what will you do with it? Run it by remote? The only person we can control is the one in the mirror, and that is 24- hour job. Discipline yourself and the world will take care of itself. Galatians 5:22

Every time I start congratulating myself about how good I am, the flesh shows up. Someone cuts me off in traffic, my neighbor's dog barks all night, a tele-marketer calls me on my cell phone, or I'm falsely accused. It's hard to understand how a Christian can become conceited and self-righteous. We pray and fast. We make a commitment to live holy all day, but before lunch, the flesh has proved us wrong. This constant war equips us to be a witness. Without it, our ministry is ineffective. Keep wrestling with the flesh. It sharpens your sword for battle. Romans 7

Forgiveness

Three of the hardest words in the English language to say are, "I was wrong." The refusal to say them has caused divorce, severed friendships, sibling rivalry, death, and even damnation. Saying these words insults the ego, admits defeat, humbles the spirit, and eliminates guilt. Set your soul and spirit free. Tell the one you love and the one you've offended that you were wrong, and watch Satan flee from behind that wall he has erected in your relationship. God requires it. 2 Corinthians 5:17-19

Just as you restart your computer, reboot your smart phone, and press the reset button on an appliance, you must do likewise with your relationships with others and the Lord. When your relationship with your significant other gets bland, boring and busted, it is time to start over. What attracted you to them in the beginning is still there, you just got used to it. Rediscover them by forgiving the past and making a commitment to the future. That's what the New Year is all about, reboot. If your joy in the Lord has weakened, your love for others has faded, and commitment to the church has lessened, reboot. Ephesians 4:23

No prophet, priest, disciple, or believer in the Bible was ever rejected by God because they sinned. The eleventh chapter of Hebrews is filled with sinners who were commended for their faith. The only people recorded in scripture who were rejected and condemned were those who rejected God first. Lesson: Never deny Truth! If you have fallen, repent, get up and keep trying. Don't turn from God under any circumstances, and He won't turn from you. 1 Samuel 15:23

When someone reminds you of your past that you have repented of, smile and show them Psalms 103:10. "He hath not dealt with us after our sins; nor rewarded us according to our iniquities. For as the heaven is high above the earth, so great is his mercy toward them that fear him. As far as the east is from the west, so far hath he removed our transgressions from us."

"I refuse to let anyone control me by letting them make me hate them." ~Dr. Martin Luther King. If someone has deceived you, used you, or hurt you, the best thing for you to do is to forgive them and keep it moving. Rest assured hate is its own reward; it corrodes the container that it is in. You only destroy yourself when you hate people. Ephesians 4:32

Friends

Don't blame anyone for treating you badly. Blame yourself for allowing them to do it. They won't answer your texts or calls. They speak in a mean tone to you when you do finally reach them. They never have anything nice to say to you, and care nothing about your feelings or opinions, but you keep trying to engage in conversation with them. Why? It's apparent they would rather have your absence than your presence, so stop punishing yourself. Leave them alone because that's exactly what they want from you. Proverbs 22:24

A real friend has your back, front and side. They'll tell you when you need a perm, a breath mint, or different shoes since the ones you're wearing don't match your outfit. They'll also tell you that the bridge is out down the road! Anyone who aids you in your vice is not your friend. Proverbs 18:24

Rather than feeling humiliated because a "friend" disappointed, deceived and defamed you by talking about you behind your back, why not rejoice? The person who did that just started to act out their real personality. They were in your corner but not on your team. Some people are in our lives for seasons and some are there for reasons. This one was seasonal. Praise God that He eliminated a burden that you didn't even know you were carrying. Proverbs 17:17

Studies show that the major key to success is being surrounded with the right people. This is a biblical concept. When Jesus started His ministry on the shores of Galilee, He handpicked his disciples one by one, not for their abilities but for their availability. Our acquaintances are predictors of our future. I can look at your posse and tell you where you will be ten years from now. We don't need faithful friends; we need friends of the faith. 1 Corinthians 15:33

"Even my close friend, someone I trusted, one who shared my bread, has turned against me." Psalms 41:9. People are a trip. They will lie on you when you are alive and lie for you when you're dead. They will criticize you when you're right and encourage you when you're wrong. They're jealous of you when you're successful but yet they'll hang around you to scoop up your leftovers. If you are a controlled by the whims of people, you're going to always be miserable because people will disappoint you. No wonder the Bible tells us to put no trust in man. Stay vision driven.

"Immediately Jesus made the disciples get into the boat and go on ahead of Him to the other side, while he dismissed the crowd." ~ Matthew 14:22. Some people you used to hang with are not around anymore, not because they forsook you, but because the Lord dismissed them. You can't get to your destiny with the wrong crowd. The Father has to filter your acquaintances. Arriving at your goals/assignment is never an accident. It requires discipline and right relationships. If some of your friends have unfriended you, deleted you from their address book and don't communicate with you anymore, don't be upset. The Lord is dismissing the crowd.

If someone says, "I'll call you" and doesn't, or "I'll get back with you," and never does, or "I'll be there and never shows up," then they don't care. People will always find time to do what they really want to do. So, the lesson is if you are a constant victim of broken promises, invest your interests elsewhere. The relationship is not reciprocal; it is actually non-existent. Let's stop wasting time on people who use us and concentrate on those who place a premium on the love we give. We spend time and money on artists, celebs, athletes, movie stars, and they don't even know we are alive. Yet we overlook those in our own house/neighborhood who are there for us when we need them. "Love begins at home and then spreads abroad." 1 Peter 4:8

Declutter your life. Clutter accumulates because we hoard things we don't need, but we refuse to discard them. It's an unpleasant eyesore, unhealthy and unusable, but we hang on to it anyway. Don't let the others' opinions weigh you down? What difference does it make if someone spoke harshly and wrongly about you who doesn't even know you? And why spend time brooding over negative comments made by people who haven't done anything with their life? Get rid of the things that are draining you of your energy that were laid on you by people who don't matter. Hebrews 12:1, 2

If you believe someone is perfect, he is not your friend. Friends share everything, even their flaws. Since we all have them, if you don't know the struggles of "your friend," he has not opened up to you. That likely means "your friend" is not comfortable enough with you to be transparent. All of us need someone we can be our true selves with, so we can confess our faults with them and pray for one another. James 5:16

Anyone who agrees with everything you say is hiding something from you. Don't trust him. Disagreements birth new ideas, new ideas invoke change, and change promotes progress. If you are having disagreements with others, listen to their side very carefully, you might learn something. Acts 15:39

Only a friend will tell you that your face is dirty. Some of what we call hating is actually loving correction from people who care about us. Listen to all critics but evaluate their critiques to see if they have malignancy attached to it. Never hate correction when it is given in the right spirit. Proverbs 15:10

"Faithful are the wounds of a friend; but the kisses of an enemy are deceitful." Proverbs 27:6. If the bridge is out down the road, you'd be less than a friend not to warn me. It may delay my arrival, but you'd save me a lot of time. If you're my enemy, you'd tell me to put the pedal to the metal which would be the end of me. We should all value people who tell us the truth, even when it hurts. They are our real friends.

Avoid people who bring out the worst in you. We tend to act differently around certain people; therefore, we all need to monitor our company and determine who inspires us to perform and act at our full potential. Find an omni-directional circle with someone to pull you down when you get too high, someone to pull you in when you get out of line, and someone to pull you up when you're down. Proverbs 17:17

Some of the people we think we can't live without are actually the ones who are keeping us from our destiny. The use of the term "my favorite" is an indication that something is wrong with our relationship with God. My favorite preacher, my favorite musician, my favorite singer, are all signals that we've put people before God. Your promotion will never occur until God is your favorite and everyone else is the supporting cast. Anything we put between us and God, we put in jeopardy. Get rid of favorites and focus on God; then your destiny will follow. Isaiah 6:1

Let's learn this. We can win more friends with our ears than with our mouths. People who listen are popular and have many friends, but the talkers among us often find themselves alone. Very few of us have learned the discipline of listening. God has designed our bodies so that our ears will never shut, but our mouths will. Your child will be a better student, your spouse can be a better mate, and your preacher a better pastor if you would only listen. But more importantly, God still speaks to us if we would take time to listen. You must pray but you also must listen. Mark 13:37

A real friend will tell you when you have spinach stuck in your teeth. A fake friend will take secret snap shots and post them on Instagram. Bullying, personal insults, rank sarcasm, and mean-spiritedness have caused some young people to commit suicide. Teach your kids how to select their friends because they can become enamored with someone who will use them as a pawn for insidious jokes. We live in serious times. Violence, cultural insensitivity, and racism are openly accepted, even among kids. They see our political leaders practicing this kind of behavior every day. Spend time with your children and monitor their friendships. Proverbs 22:6

Some of us have our enemies on speed dial and have assigned them a special ring. The trouble is we don't realize it. The reason we don't realize they are detrimental to us is that the timing is not right. God teaches us through unfaithful relationships that only He can be trusted, not people. We must often learn the hard way that we can't feed a rabid dog and expect him to be loyal to us. The good news is that even when we have been deceived, it pushes us to our destiny. Be kind to everyone you meet but put your trust only in God. Psalms 41:9

Funerals

Pulpit/Pew Etiquette 101:

1. If you are asked to speak three minutes at a funeral, don't speak five and charge the rest to the Holy Spirit. It wasn't Him.
2. If you are asked to sing, don't do a concert.
3. Don't hold trivial conversations in the pulpit while the family is grieving.
4. Never tell the family, "I know how you feel." You don't.

5.   Keep it simple. All of us will face the terrible day when we will lay loved ones to rest.

Just imagine if the situation was reversed. That will help you make wise decisions as to how to behave at a funeral. Hebrews 10:24

Future

Start acting like your tomorrow today. Don't wait until God gives you a new home to actually clean the one you have, keep the one you're in clean today. If you're expecting God to give you a Cadillac tomorrow, go change the oil in your Toyota, wash it and Amor All the tires today. If you're expecting your husband to show up tomorrow, you can't walk around in Wal-Mart in your pajamas today. If you want a promotion on your job tomorrow, go to work on time today. It's just that simple. Some of our blessings are hindered for tomorrow because we have neglected today. Ecclesiastes 11:1

If you are tired of re-runs, change the channel. If you are seeing the same thing today that you saw last year this time, more than likely you are still thinking and behaving like you were last year at this time. Some habits, people and places must be left behind in order to see a brighter future. Liars lie, cheaters cheat, and thieves steal and no one has ever won the Kentucky Derby with a mule. Change your environment and your future will follow. Romans 7:6

Giving to Leadership

Do you need a financial, physical or spiritual blessing? Do you want to get God's undivided attention? Is there something from which you need deliverance? It's easy to get it. You don't need to play the number you dreamed about, consult the Zodiac, or get advice from a palm reader. Here's what you do. Write your pastor a check. That's right. Send him a card of appreciation for his leadership. After you give them the check, submit to their spiritual leadership. God said it. I didn't. Read Galatians 6:6- 7; 1 Timothy 5:17-20.

God's Goodness

Nothing good happens when people try to hold on to something they already possess. Someone reading this message is absolutely miserable because you're trying to hold on to someone or something that God doesn't want you to have. It's a biblical fact that anything God wants you to have can't be lost. If you lose anything as a believer, it wasn't yours in the beginning. Let it/them go. If God wants you to have it, it will come back to you even better than before. Matthew 10:39

Reminding someone of how bad he is will only push him further away from you and God. People are not ignorant of their sins and faults. Every one of us knows exactly when we did wrong and who we offended. Reminding someone of how good God is brings him to repentance. This doesn't negate the fact that people should see themselves as sinners. Beating them over the head with the Bible only shows the shallowness of the one who's witnessing. Tell someone how good God is today. Romans 2:4

Don't mistake God's goodness with your current condition. God is not only good when you get that job. He's good when you are unemployed. He's not only good when you get healed. He's good when you are sick. He's not only good when the money rolls in. He's good when you're broke. Goodness is not what He does, it's His nature. When life is not good for you, know this; God is looking forward to your future to make you good. Romans 8:28

Aren't you glad God doesn't hold grudges? Some people will never forget what you did and will snub you to no end. They will constantly remind you of how you hurt them, even when you have asked them for forgiveness. But God doesn't pout. He waits patiently for us to take ownership of our mistakes, and then He renews us. Yesterday means "yes to today." Learn from the past but live for tomorrow. Philippians 3:13, 14

God is not broke. Whatever He gives you takes nothing away from me. God has an unlimited supply of blessings. Sometimes God gives us material possessions to reveal our devotion to Him. What Benny Hinn, Creflo Dollar, and Kenneth Copeland have is of no concern to another Christian. Be faithful to God with what He has given you. Let's be careful and examine our own hearts to make sure that our motivation for serving the Lord is not what He gives, but who He is. 1 Timothy 6:6-12

I've heard it said that if God had a refrigerator, your name and address would be on it. If God had a wallet, your picture would be in it. Don't let anyone tell you that God doesn't love you. He loves you in spite of anything you've done in your past. I heard a preacher say this weekend that God wants to love you. It broke my heart to hear such a misinterpretation of God's Word. There is no requirement for God's love. He loves us because He is love. Whatever you're facing today, hold your head up, and rejoice in the God of love. Romans 5:8

A one-hundred-pound derelict and a one-hundred-and-fifty-pound scientist weigh the same thing on God's scale. God doesn't value us according to what we do or what we have. We are all equal in His sight. We don't have to be "good" for God to love us; He loves us because He is good. Hold your head up today and be faithful to God in your calling. He loves you. If your assignment is ushering at the church door, your faithfulness guarantees you the same reward as Billy Graham. Revelations 2:10

Your conception may have been an accident. Even if your parents didn't plan their pregnancy, your birth was not a mistake. God knows you and loves you just as you are. He has a purpose for you. To find that purpose, establish an earnest, routine, and constant practice of worship. God will speak to you and clearly delineate the reason for your being alive. That's when joy will flood your soul. The most joyful people on the planet are the ones who know their purpose. Jeremiah 1:5

God's Presence

Since we are made in God's image, it is evident that God has emotions. Did you know that God can be grieved? Ephesians 4:30. God can be happy. Psalm 34:1. He loves. 1 John 4:11. He can hate. Proverbs 6:16. He can feel pain. Isaiah 42:14. He can cry. John 11:35, and He can get angry. Psalms 30:5. Does that mean God is human? No, it simply means we ought to consider God's feelings in everything we do and treat Him like our best friend.

Beautiful places are not enjoyable unless you're with the right person. Who wants to go to Hawaii, Greece, Aruba, or Riviera by themselves? Imagine going to the most exotic place in the world alone and with no camera. It's no fun. But now imagine being with someone you love and who loves you. You see, joy is not found in places but in people. The greatest promise in the Bible is not healing, prosperity, or victory over enemies. It is the promise of the presence of God. When God is with you, the place doesn't matter. Whatever you're facing today, know this. Believer, God is with you. Hebrews 13:5

Gossip

Never entertain backbiting, berating or belittling of another person. When someone approaches you with hearsay about someone, it is always because they don't feel good about themselves. For them to feel better about themselves, they will attempt to devalue another. They somehow think their actions place them on a higher pedestal than the other person. Don't let them use your ears as garbage cans so they can justify their own self-serving inadequacies. When they have finished with that person, they will be on their merry way to their next victim to tear you down. Backbiting in Romans 1:30 is placed in the same category as "haters of God." Don't do it or entertain it.

It appears that people who have done evil are less forgiving, less compassionate, and more judgmental of others who have fallen, than those who don't have a checkered past. Since God has forgiven you of so much, why not extend that same kind of compassion to struggling Christians who are wrestling with strong-holds. Put weak Christians on your prayer list, not your billboard. Matthew 18:27-29

What if you had a doctor who made a diagnosis all the time and never wrote a prescription? What would you do? Isn't it strange how we can identify the problems in other people's lives, but never offer a solution to them? If I'm wrong, come talk to me and help me get it right. It doesn't help when you permeate the community with your assumptions about how bad I am. Help me. The best way to help me is to start by looking in the mirror. Matthew 7:3

One day while I was running, I saw a buzzard get hit by a car while eating road-kill. It reminded me of people who have a hunger for gossip. Flocking to gossip mongers for the latest gossip on others will ultimately result in your own demise. An old church mother used to tell us that the same dog that brings a bone will take one. Translation: An individual who shares gossip with you will gossip about you. When someone comes to you with the latest "news," simply grab them by the hand and say, "Let's pray about it." They will never bring gossip to you again. Proverbs 16:28

"And that ye study to be quiet, and to do your own business, and to work with your own hands, as we commanded you." And the Lord drops the mic and walks off the stage. 1 Thessalonians 4:11

Now that you know my business, what are you going to do with it? You've Googled me, asked my friends surreptitious questions and you've even driven through my neighborhood. Now what? All you can do now is talk. Is that going to help you? Listen. I'm a mess and so are you, so since we both know that, let's stop snooping on each other and work on ourselves. You take care of you and I'll do my best to take care of me. Agreed? "And that ye study to be quiet, and to do your own business, and to work with your own hands, as we commanded you." 1 Thessalonians 4:11

Everyone reading this message has been impacted negatively by hearsay and gossip. People are quick to believe a lie before even considering the source that brings the information. We often wonder why an acquaintance stops speaking or the person you just met gives you a cold shoulder or even why close relatives no longer want to be around. It's because of something they heard. Make a mental note. Before you receive any communication from anyone about someone, examine the one who's doing the talk. No one who is right with the Lord enjoys tearing down someone else. Proverbs 16:28

The best way to judge a person is not by what others say about them, but by what they say about others. When someone always talks negatively, points an accusing finger, and finds fault in other people, it is a testimony of his character. We usually see things, not as they are, but as we are. Listen carefully to those who want to gain your company so you may observe their attitude toward others. You might save yourself a lot of agony and grief in future relationships. Job 1

Grace

No one cares how much you know until they know how much you care. One of the most difficult tasks in life is listening. Many people you meet today need a listening ear. Be careful not to be critical and judgmental because were it not for God's matchless grace, the person you are talking to could be you. 1 John 3:14-18

We should never be ashamed of who we are if we're saved. Everything we've gone through has made us who we are and it all was permitted by God. He has taken all that the enemy has thrown at us and given us a testimony. What the devil meant for evil, God will turn around for good. He has given us lemonade from lemons, wine from crushed grapes and a garment of praise for ashes. Hold your head high because we've been hand crafted by divinity. 1 Corinthians 15:10

May the works I've done speak for me. May the service I give speak for me. When I'm resting in my grave, and there's nothing that can be said, may the works I've done speak for me. These are classic lyrics, but it is bad theology. We shouldn't trust the best ten minutes we've ever lived to get us into heaven. We should want the blood of Jesus to speak for us. That's the only thing God will accept at the judgment. There needs to be more preaching about the blood and less about us. Romans 5:9

Praise God for His grace. You wouldn't be able to wear a silk tie/scarf with a cotton shirt/blouse and you wouldn't be permitted to watch college football on Saturdays under the law. Women couldn't wear pants and males would be responsible for all unwed females in their family. Lastly, any prophet who made a prediction that didn't come to pass would be stoned to death. Preachers you ought to shout on that last one. How wonderful was that cross! Galatians 3:24-29

The term "amazing grace" is redundant. Grace doesn't need a qualifier. It's amazing all by itself. All we need is a good memory to understand how amazing grace really is. We are sinners by birth, choice and nature, but in spite of our sinfulness, God gives us new life. That's amazing! Want to celebrate freedom? Thank God you are no longer in bondage to sin. Ephesians 2:8

We should be glad the Son of God was made in the "likeness" of men and not like men. What if God was like men? Many of us would not have gotten out of bed this morning because we wouldn't be able to afford it. If God were like men, air would be taxed and sunlight would be available for only a few. If God were like men those of us who don't believe in Him wouldn't have food or shelter. If God were like men anyone who opposed Him would be imprisoned, killed and banished from the face of the Earth. If God were like men, the church would be filled every Sunday because we would be too afraid to miss. Thank goodness that God is not like men. He is full of love and mercy and gives us a choice to serve Him. Choose to serve Him. Philippians 2:7

"Whoever attempts to hold me hostage to my history, good luck!" ~Rev. Tellis Chapman. Guilt is unnecessary because forgiveness is available through Jesus Christ. There's no reason for anyone to walk around in a prison of guilt. Every person in the world is about 18 inches from a clear conscience. All we have to do is fall on our knees and receive it. Don't spend another day in misery, being depressed, and or contemplating suicide. Repent and let the peace of God overflow your soul. God loves you in spite of what you've done, and He wants to set you free, just receive it by faith. Lamentations 3:22, 23

Don't dare give up on people who seem to be incorrigible. Many of us have quit praying for a family member, classmate or co-worker because we think there's no use. Don't ever forget your condition before your conversion. Some of us were drug addicts, gamblers, fornicators, and liars, but God's grace reached us. That's something we should never forget. The further we sink in sin, the greater the testimony of His grace. If God forgave, regenerated, and restored you, don't you think He can do it for others? Keep praying, witnessing, and loving folks, especially those for whom you feel there's no hope. 1 Corinthians 6:9-11

I'm constantly reminded of my sinfulness every day. When someone cuts me off in traffic, when trouble enters the life of someone who hurt me, or when a beautiful woman walks by, all these things bring me back to reality and scream in my ear, "You're human Ronnie!" No amount of church attendance, fasting and praying, reading and reciting scripture will take away your humanity. If it did, we could glory in our works and human efforts and then take credit for our salvation. Thank God for His grace! All our glorying in self or flesh is vain, but we can take comfort in God's mercy through His Grace. Romans 5:19-21

We can all agree that favor isn't fair, but many of us use this idea to imply that God caters to us more than He does to other believers. Let's never forget that God is not a respecter of persons. Favor isn't fair because the term "fair" is a legal term which means you will get what you deserve. In that regard, none of us should want God to be fair. All of us should prefer grace. We all are sinners, but the truth is that everyone reading this message can have favor if they open their heart to His Son. When we become Children of God, all of us have favor through His grace. Romans 2:11

Happiness

Happiness is not something you find, it's something you create. As an artist starting with a blank canvas takes his skillful hand and ends up with a masterpiece, so must we begin with what we have to formulate a happy life. The canvas you begin with is you. You must like yourself first. The only way to like you is to accept yourself like God made you. It's not in money, materialism and people; it's in being comfortable with yourself. You'll never be happy looking outside of yourself. The voice of more must be silenced in your head and replaced with the voice of the Holy Spirit. Open your heart today and let Him dwell in you. Philippians 4:4-7

Happiness is a state of mind that can only be derived by being thankful. Show me a thankful person, and I will show you a happy person. Show me an unthankful person, and I will show you an unhappy person. Our thankfulness enhances our praise. It is impossible to praise the Lord with an unthankful heart. Let's not let our circumstances and situations determine our thanksgiving. When Paul spoke from a Roman prison, he said, "I think myself happy." Philippians 4:11

Helpful hint for a happy day: Don't let mean people spoil your day. You can meet people in the mall that you go to church with and they will pretend that they don't see you. Don't let that dampen your spirit; keep smiling. There's nothing you can do to change a person's personality. The Holy Spirit doesn't do it, so you know you can't do it either. Do the next best thing—be kind to them and keep walking, you'll live longer. Ephesians 4:32

The desire to be happy is a God-given instinct and a longing for the presence of God. We unwittingly search for happiness in things, people and positions, but the only thing that will fill the hole in our souls is God. Don't criticize the alcoholic and addict. Love them because they were misled into thinking that they could find heaven in a bottle or pipe. A Christian is simply a person who got it right by following the unction of the Holy Spirit. Never judge addicts of any kind. Have compassion on them because were it not for the grace of God, there go us. Ephesians 2:8, 9

We stay up late and get up early. We drink out of a plastic bottle filled with water that probably came from someone's bath tub. We order breakfast, lunch and dinner by a number from the front seat of our car, and drive while we eat. We talk for hours a day on a radioactive device to family and friends or text them while in bumper to bumper traffic. We won't go to the doctor until we see blood coming from an orifice of our body. We take meds to go to sleep, meds to wake up, meds to slow down, and meds to speed up. All of this, and we have the nerve to say that rats are in a race. Maybe rats are in a people race. Take your time and enjoy your life. Ecclesiastes 3:12-14

The key to happiness is being content with oneself. If we look to people and things to make us happy, we will always be disappointed. The only thing we can control in this world is ourselves. We have no power over our surroundings; therefore, we should not look around us for emotional support. Look inward to the Holy Spirit. He makes us comfortable in our own skin and blesses us with contentment. Philippians 4:11-13

A string of cars was in front of me. I didn't know why, but gradually cars passed a moped that was holding up the traffic. When I approached, I saw a man and a woman smiling and talking as if no one else in the world existed. I passed them, too, and came to a traffic light where I saw a couple in a Lincoln seemingly arguing. The woman was pointing her finger at the man as he looked out of the window to ignore her. I was reminded that it's not what you have or who you are that will make you happy. Rather, your happiness hinges on who has you and whether you like yourself. That makes all the difference in the world. To be happy, do not add to your possessions, but subtract from your desires. If you don't enjoy what you have, how could you be happier with more? Ecclesiastes 9:9

Hate

Are you sure they are hating on you? They may be helping you. Why spend so much time worrying about what people say about you or what they did to you? A thirty second conversation can ruin an entire day for some of us because we're thinking about what was said about us. Stop concentrating on them and focus on Him. God uses everybody, even mean folk. He uses them to show us His glory. Your haters help you to get to your destiny. Matthew 26:50

It's not always that people don't understand what you're saying. Most times they just don't like you. Have you noticed that if you like someone, you tend to agree with everything the person says, but if you don't care that much for them, nothing they do is right? The scribes and Pharisees claimed they couldn't understand Jesus, but they crucified him because they simply didn't like him. Lesson: If you don't have critics, you don't have a ministry. Stop arguing with your haters because you'll never convince them to see your way of thinking. Instead, concentrate on being amenable to the Holy Spirit instead. Luke 6:1-12

Why are you preoccupied with thoughts about your haters? Birds fly. Fish swim. Dogs bark, and haters hate. That's what they do. It's not you in particular; they hate on everybody. Why are you surprised? Learn to treat them like landscape. Admire them from a distance and keep going because ultimately, all they can do is make your life more beautiful. God has sufficiently given each of us some haters. They are not to destroy us but to elevate us. Rejoice and be exceedingly glad when your enemy attacks. Psalms 41:5-11

Hate is a terrible vice that acts like a boomerang. If you hate homosexuals, somewhere down the road, you're going to have someone homosexual in your family. If you hate white people, sooner or later, someone you love is going to marry a white person. If you hate black people, well you get the message. God will never let us get away with hate because it is the exact opposite of Him. God is love. "I refuse to let someone pull me down below them by making me hate them." ~Dr. Martin Luther King. Genesis 29:31

Hate will destroy you from the inside out. If you have been hurt by anything or anybody, chalk it up to being human. It's a part of life. Anyone you have ill feelings for reveals something about you not them. They do what comes naturally to them and when you get angry, you become the victim. Learn to live free of the control of others. Ephesians 4:32

The Holy Spirit

The difference between a brick and a basketball is what's on the inside. If you throw a brick into water, it sinks and stays. If you throw a basketball into water, it comes to the top. We have someone on the inside who won't let us stay down. The Holy Ghost always causes us to bounce back. He is the lifter of our heads. Psalms 3:3

We all have contented passengers on life's bus as long as they can dictate the course of the journey from behind. As soon as we start directing our own destiny and refuse advice from back seat drivers, they will want to get off at the next bus stop. Advice: Pull over. Let all of them off and charge them no fare because they were not for you in the beginning. Jesus had twelve followers with Him. Judas was a backseat driver who got mad because he could not determine the trip. Let's stay in tune with the Holy Spirit and stop entertaining comments from those who want to lead from behind. Romans 8:14

The Holy Spirit wants to cover you. The devil wants to accuse you before God and men. The term devil means "slanderer." Whenever we hear negative things about each other, true or untrue, if the impulse is to spread it, it's of the devil. We should cover each other for the sake of the entire Body of Christ and attempt to personally and privately restore the fallen saint. If you are publishing on Facebook or laughing and talking about a fallen Christian, you're doing the devil's work. Everyone who does the devil's work will receive the devil's pay. Let's never rejoice at the fall of another believer but pray for restoration instead. None of us are above a fall. Galatians 6:1

The Holy Spirit will never distract, interfere or prevent preaching. Saying "Amen" means I believe this is true, but yelling, shouting and dancing over preaching is not of the Holy Spirit. All this may be in order after the sermon is finished, but to do this while the Word goes forth serves only to draw attention. The Holy Spirit is a gentleman and does everything decently and in order. Let's be careful not to let Satan deceive us into thinking that fanaticism is of the Spirit. 1 Corinthians 14:40

A homeless guy walked up to me at Ingles and asked for money. He said he needed $8.15 to buy something to eat for him and his wife. At the time I only had a twenty, so I told him to wait until I came back out of the store. When I got back, he was waiting, but I changed my mind because I felt he was trying to get money for wine. Sure enough, he took the money others had given him and walked across the street to the ABC store. Be led by the Spirit when giving on the street. Not only is it dangerous, but it enables addicts. Some beggars are really needy, but others will play on your emotions. Romans 8:14

The Holy Ghost didn't tell you to yell over the preacher when he stood to preach. Neither did He tell you to speak 15 minutes at the funeral when you were asked to give remarks for two minutes. The Holy Spirit was not in your dance when you knocked over that little old lady. The Holy Ghost had nothing to do with you telling anybody anything that is not in the Scriptures. The Holy Ghost is the most lied on individual in the world, and it is done by those who claim to love Him. Let's be careful not to attribute our bad habits to the sweet Holy Spirit. 1 Corinthians 14:40

Just walked away with a warm feeling after feeding a homeless family in Augusta, GA. Suddenly, the Holy Spirit reminded me that they will be hungry again in a couple of hours. What they needed was not a hand out but a hand up. The Church has the power to change the world, but we are stuck in our selfishness. Many of us are competing to see who is "Sunday's Best." The Church could eliminate hunger in America if we all gave up some creature comforts and developed a spiritual sensitivity toward the needs of others. Enough with ecclesiastical consumerism, let's look around for opportunities to produce Kingdom minded communities. Matthew 16:19

The anointing is attractive. When God gives you an assignment, He equips you to do it by anointing you with the Holy Spirit. You have a supernatural magnetic appeal that cannot be explained in earthly terms. Some people gravitate towards you like a moth to a flame. Others flee like house flies from a fly swat. Others attack you because of envy. It is not you. It is the God in you they reject. No progressive, anointed, and effective ministry is exempt from attacks. If you are under attack, it is because of your attractiveness, and it is an indication that you are on the right track. Stay the course. John 7:1-9

Arguing is stressful and frustrating and only occurs when neither party concedes. The arguing stops if one of the persons in the quarrel relents and agrees with the other. The accompanying stress and frustration leave too. Many of us are depressed and filled with anxiety because our spirit is in an argument with the Holy Spirit. The Holy Spirit is telling us we're wrong and we're saying to Him we're right. When we agree with the Holy Spirit, the anxiety and frustration disappear because there's no more arguing within. That's what confession means, "agreeing with God." 1 John 1:9

Hope

When it is night in China, it is day in the U.S. When it's dark on the east coast, it may be light on the west coast because the world spins on its axis, and time zones have been put in place to regulate daylight. It may be dark in your life today, believer, but don't give up hope, the world is still turning. On the other hand, you may be on top of the world today, but tomorrow the world could be on top of you. The good news is that God rules, so trust Him. Psalms 30:5

Most men have three wishes. They desire to outsmart the lottery, attract women and catch fish. They have proven to be unsuccessful in every case. There is a difference between wishing and hope. Wishing is based on chance, and hope is based in the Word of God. Leave wishing for fishing and hope for living. No matter how dark it is for you today, there's hope in Christ. Hope is faith holding its hand out in the dark. "If God said it, I believe it, and that settles it." The truth is, if God said it that settles it whether you believe it or not. Mark 13:31

Hospital Etiquette

1. If you visit someone in the hospital and he is asleep, don't wake him up. You don't know how long it took them to fall to sleep or how many people have visited them before you.
2. Don't set up camp. Only stay a few minutes unless they want you to stay longer. Be conscious of the fact that they are not there to entertain you but to get well.
3. No yelling in your prayer. There are other people in the facility besides the one you're praying for. Besides, God is not deaf. Whispering is okay.
4. Don't ask them how they are feeling. Can you imagine how many times they have told visitors the same story? They will tell you if they want you to know. It's all about using common sense. Be courteous. Galatians 5:22

Humility

The higher a monkey climbs up a tree, the more his business is exposed. Therefore, it is a smart monkey who invests in trousers. If you are moving up the social ladder and you're being blessed by the Lord to acquire success, don't forget where you came from or the people who helped you get there. The same things you see going up are the things you will see when you are on your way down. It's pure Christianity to help the people you left behind. Mark 6:1

In "The Color Purple," when Celie walked up the porch to shave Mister, many of us were shouting, "Cut him!" If we aren't careful, people will pull us down to their level. When you hear what they say about you and see their attempts to hurt you, don't retaliate. Take the high road. There are less pot holes, speed traps and crossing animals. Christians follow Christ. Therefore, we must respond to attacks the way He did. We never see Jesus doing an "eye for an eye." Getting even puts us beneath our enemy; let God fight your battles. God affords us many opportunities to display Christian values. You may face one today. Avoid the low road. Matthew 5:38-48

We are addicted to power; therefore, we compete with each other to see who's the best. We try to discover who is the strongest man, who is the fastest, who is the best gamer, who is the brightest, and the most talented. People want strong partners who are self-sufficient, self-confident and self-reliant. God is totally opposite from us. He wants the weak, the helpless and pitiful. What often hinders our deliverance is our strength. Many of us are too strong to be delivered, so God waits until we've exhausted all our resources before He comes to rescue us. Why not humble yourself and submit to His authority and save yourself a lot of anxiety? 2 Corinthians 12:7-10

The key to God's heart is to take the low road. When we put others before ourselves, we please God. When we put things and ourselves before people, we displease God. Being a Christian is more than church membership; it's serving others. If you don't like people, re-evaluate your relationship with God because we were placed here to serve not to be served. Ask yourself this question: If no one ever recognizes me for what I do for the Kingdom, will I still do it? Your answer determines your level of devotion to God. James 4:6, 10

Take the low road so that when you fail, people will be there for you and have compassion on you. No one cares how good you are at what you do, how much you own, or how perfect your life is right now. Take off your golden shoes. People know better. You can never go wrong being the real you. That way you'll never have to remember who you were the last time we met. Matthew 23:12

"Speak softly and carry a big stick" ~ Theodore Roosevelt. Last night LeBron James blocked Steph Curry's layup under the goal and then turned to him "jaw jacking." What kind of message does that send to little kids watching the game? Our youth idolize athletes and will imitate them on the basketball court. Broadcasters and sportswriters should consider James' attitude when making their decision for the MVP award. It is never good sportsmanship to humiliate the loser. Greatness is not just physical, but mental also. We must win with humility.

All of us have cracks in our armor, but don't show them to your enemies. Lesson: Keep cool. Stay humble and keep smiling. When you are provoked, they won't know if they are getting to you. We have all been tested by co-workers, family and even fellow Christians. Hang in there. Don't reveal the crack in your armor. 1 Corinthians 13:5

Humility is a strange thing. The minute we know we have it, we've just lost it. If we ask God to give it to us, He has to break us. When we try to catch it, it slips right out of our hands like a greased pig. It is something we must have to get our prayers answered, but very few of us have it. It only comes when we allow ourselves to get pinned by the weight of the world, and we completely surrender, and place ourselves in the hand s of God. At that point, we don't care what people think. Our eyes are sharply focused on God. Humble yourself today. Don't wait for God to do it for you. James 4:10

Jealousy

Jealousy has no place among believers. If God has blessed your neighbor, He is in the neighborhood. If He is in the neighborhood, He can stop by your house. The best way to get more from God is to praise Him for what He has done for someone else. Romans 12:15

Joy

I always wondered why the Bible says, "The joy of the Lord is your strength" rather than "The Lord is the strength of your joy" until I found out that the word "joy" in that text means "wall." Nehemiah was rebuilding a wall to protect the people from the enemy and he uses a pun to say your "joy" will protect you from your spiritual foes. We have a wall in our joy. Nehemiah 8:10

Holiness is not in a hole, it's in your joy. Christians aren't happy all the time, but we ought to have joy 24/7 because it is a fruit of the Spirit. Wearing colonial clothing and religious head dress, forsaking technical accoutrements, distancing yourself from mainstream Christianity and looking like a turkey in November, do not make one holy. I've met some of the meanest people who believe they can achieve a right relationship with God by denying their humanity and posturing as icons of perfection. It isn't so. They say, "I don't smoke, drink or chew." Neither does a flag pole, but that doesn't make it holy. Our strength is in our joy: let's pray for it. Nehemiah 8:9-12

Judging

Let's face it. We often judge people by how they look, what they have, and how talented/athletic they are. Focusing on these superficial things causes us to overlook many who would bless our lives. God often sends what we need in strange packages. That's what Christmas is about. The very thing the world needed came in a manger from the

womb of a virgin wrapped in rags. The next time you snob somebody, remember, that may be just the one you need to bless you.
1 Corinthians 1:27-31

I was thinking about trading cars, and I noticed that the dealership judged my trade-in out of one book and their car out of another. Their car, according to them, is worth a lot more than mine even though I only had 60,000 miles on it. Unless you know cars really well, you couldn't tell the difference between the two. Aren't you glad that God will judge us all out of the same Book? There will be no double standard in the judgment, and no one will get a "hook-up." The good news is that you can settle out of court. There is an advocate, "lawyer," who is willing to take your case. Having Jesus to represent you eliminates The Great White Throne Judgment. Hebrews 7:25

I had a long drive to Danville, VA, so I didn't shave. I put on an old T-shirt and worn jeans. I figured I wouldn't stop but for gas. When I arrived at the hotel the receptionist didn't even make eye contact. She handed me my room key, and I went up to get dressed for church. When I came back down the elevator, she was smiling, as she said, "You clean up well." I am the same person in jeans as I am in a suit, but people view me differently based on what I am wearing. I have some food for thought. How many people have we overlooked and ostracized because of the way they are dressed? Judging according to appearance is a shallow trait that causes us to miss many contributions that others can add to our lives. Stop looking over people. The one you look over may be the one the Lord sent to bless you. 1 Samuel 16:7

The most valuable lesson I've learned in my 40 years of ministry is never to judge anyone by what someone else says about them. Just because two people had bad chemistry between them doesn't mean the same will happen with you. Some of us belittle, berate, and begrudge others because it makes us feel better about our own shortcomings.

Give everyone you meet a chance. You may find a lifetime friendship with someone you heard negative things about. Psalm 31:18

By the world's standards, Jesus was a complete failure. He didn't own a home. He had no transportation or money, and He was hated by the majority of the populace. He was sentenced, condemned, and executed in a place that carried the worst stigma in town while all His friends forsook Him. However, by God's standards he was a total success because he completely accomplished his assignment. Never judge people for what they have. Judge them by their faithfulness and commitment to principle. John 5:29-31

Sometimes we judge people we meet precipitously because of their facial expression. I met someone yesterday and assumed he was unfriendly because of the indifference I saw on his face. When I spoke to him, immediately his face lit up, and we had a very enjoyable conversation. I learned a lesson. Never assume people are unfriendly because of their facial expressions. You never know what people are dealing with. They may just need a kind word to cheer them up. Proverbs 18:24

Pointing out how wrong I am still doesn't make what you did right. We both were wrong. This argument is called ad hominem in ethics. It focuses on attacking another's character rather than dealing with the issue at hand. When we all stand before God, He's not going to ask you what others did. He's going to judge you for your own works. Put down the telescope and pick up a mirror. 2 Corinthians 5:10

Kindness

God doesn't see us for what we are but for what we could be. He sees the "best" in us. We see from the beginning to the end, but God sees the end first and then works towards the beginning. Shouldn't we do the same with each other? Let's stop viewing each other as suspects and take what we see in one another at face value. We can start by simply finding something good about the next person we see and complimenting them. There's something good you can say about everyone. John 13:15

If you greet someone and the person doesn't return your salutation, you can't refuse to speak him. If you only respond to how you are treated, that first person controls you. People can control our behavior if we allow their negative attitude and indifference into our spirit. Be yourself. Be kind and courteous regardless how others treat you. It frees you from the control of mean-spirited people. Romans 12:10

Law

The law ensures that we do what's right, but we shouldn't do what's right just because it's the law. The law says if we make a baby we must take care of that baby, but we shouldn't need the law to force us to provide for our kids. We should support our children because we love them. When we are governed only by the law, we must be watched because we will break the law when given the opportunity. When we are guided by love, there's no need for the law. Galatians 3:24, 25

Leaders

You wouldn't get on a plane with a pilot who has never studied the craft and art of flying. You wouldn't take medicine prepared by a pharmacist who has not been trained, and you surely wouldn't let a doctor operate on you who has never held a scalpel. To be certified in any field of discipline, one must "ride in the second chariot" to get training for that vocation. The rules seem to apply in every field except ministry. Many ministries today have no covering because the leader won't sit still long enough to get prepared. Therefore, people are confused because ministers are not properly prepared. Christians, examine your leader's credentials. 2 Timothy 2:15

God never uses volunteers. He only uses the draft system. Not one prophet, patriarch or disciple in Bible volunteered. God calls, chooses, and then equips His soldiers to do battle. Be very wary of those who want to be in charge. Every one of God's leaders was handpicked by Him and then given enjoyment for the assignment later. He placed each one of them in a servile position first, and then advanced them to leadership. If you are not willing to serve, you are not fit to be a leader. Mark 10:35-45

God reveals things to leaders that He doesn't share with the whole group. Your bus driver can see much better than the guy in the back seat, and leaders can see a lot clearer than followers. Would it make sense to rise up from the back of a bus and start choking the driver? If you don't respect the driver, get off the bus. Pray for your leaders; respect and honor them. They were placed in position to serve you. Romans 13

We can't control the lives of our grown children. At some point our leadership style must change. If a sapling begins to lean, we can keep it straight by tying three cords on either side of it. When kids are young, we must use discipline, love, and be a good example to keep them straight. When they are fully grown, there's nothing we can do but admire their beauty and usefulness. It is futile to treat an adult like a three- year- old. We can only offer advice and pray that they will listen to season. Let your adult kids live their own lives. Proverbs 29:17

He changes the seasons and guides history. He raises up kings and also brings them down. He provides both intelligence and discernment. He opens up the depths, tells secrets, and sees in the dark. Light spills out of him! ~Daniel 2:21. Folks, relax. God's got this.

You did all you could do when you went to the polls. God gives us leaders that we deserve and this is what America has earned. The Earth is the Lord's, not (your name here). He is still in charge, and we are just passengers on His bus. Sit back, chill and enjoy the ride. It's going to be a doozy.

Pastors: Take nothing under the table. If anyone comes to you in your ministry and hands you something they want to keep a secret, you become complicit in their scheming. It's understandable that some believers don't want to be called out or recognized for what they do but be careful about receiving secret gifts. Anyone who wants to give under the table wants you under the table as well. Keep everything above the table and you won't lose your seat at the table. 2 Corinthians 8:21

Nothing you give to your spiritual leader is wasted. God has promised to bless you when you are sensitive to the needs of your preacher. Go to your pastor Sunday and hand him a gift, just because, and watch God bless you. Galatians 6:6-7

A good mentor is not someone who wants to keep you under his thumb, but someone who prepares you to stand on your own feet. Be careful of people who are simply trying to control you and use you to do their bidding. If your leader is not Kingdom minded, find another one who is interested in developing you for the use of the Master, not his/her own. Anyone can create "yes-men," but it takes a Spirit-filled leader to launch ministers and ministries. Ephesians 4:11-12

Leadership is not just identifying the problems but devising plans to correct them. Leadership is not pointing out who is at fault but taking responsibility for your role as the leader. Leadership means taking a little more than your share of the blame and a little less of your share of the credit. America is in dire straits today because our leaders have more nightmares than dreams and are more interested in the fleece than the flock. Every day the headlines reveal a new calamity in Washington. How much more can we take? Pray for America. 1 Timothy 2:1-3

The Church has two kinds of leaders, those who are interested in the fleece and those who are interested in the flock. The two are easily distinguishable. The fleece chaser is always interested in his profit, his performance, and his pride. Those leaders who are interested in the flock focus on the will of the Shepherd, His sayings, and His sovereignty. Listen very carefully to your pastor; you might learn something. The Lord's sheep should know His voice. John 10:4-6

Listening

The experts told the Wright Brothers that if a man was meant to fly, "He would have been born with wings." They also told Henry Ford, "If you succeed in building that thing, there are no roads to drive it on." The experts say that a bumble bee isn't supposed to fly. If you listen to the experts you'll never do anything but sit, soak and sour. "Ex" means out and "Pert" means to drip. Question: Why listen to a one who drips out information when we have a fountain available? Genesis 18:14

To be honest, sometimes I watch NFL games with my TV on mute because I really don't need John Gruden, Trent Dilfer or Chris Berman to tell me what I just saw with my own eyes. Try it sometimes and your perspective of the game will be a lot different. Listening to someone else's opinion about something can alter your opinion about the very thing you saw. Let's never allow other people to color our views of people. Treat people like you want to be treated, regardless to what others say about them. Luke 6:31

If multiple people in your past have told you the same things about yourself, they can't all be wrong. Maybe you should listen. We don't like to face reality about ourselves, so we shrug it off by saying, "They just don't like me." No, they may be right. Everyone can't be wrong. There is always discomfort before development, pain before productivity, and anguish before improvement. To become better people, we have to acknowledge our faults even when it hurts. James 5:16

There's a time to speak and there's a time to keep silent, but the hardest thing in the world to do is to keep silent. Have you ever been talking to someone when they finished your sentence for you? Isn't that annoying? I watched with amazement as a group of ladies walked down the street together and every one of them was talking at the same time. Is that communication? As Christians, let's be sensitive to other's opinions and be less dogmatic. The truth doesn't have to be shouted, repeated, or forced. It stands all by itself and doesn't need our help. Listen more than you speak; you will be appreciated a lot more. Ecclesiastes 3:7

If you want someone to remember something you have to say, whisper it to the person. You must be close to someone to whisper in his war. The person must also listen attentively. Yelling is threatening and a sign of insecurity. Satan shouts at us; God whispers. If there is a thunderous voice shouting at you today, don't listen. When you are all alone, God speaks softly and tenderly because He wants our undivided attention. Listen to His voice. 1 Kings 19:12

It appears that this generation is the only one that scoffs at the advice of their elders. Yes, you have the internet and social media and you can Google anything that comes to mind. However, the information you get makes you less capable of thinking. Try going to your grandparents. They may think slower than you, but they think a lot deeper. My dad was the most insightful, witty, and resourceful man I've ever known, but he never finished the sixth grade. There is more information buried in our cemeteries than we have in our libraries. Spend some time at Grandma's house. Proverbs 5:1-2

No one ever listened themselves out of a job, listened themselves into a black eye, or even listened themselves into a speeding ticket. God designed our bodies so that our ears will not shut up but our mouths will. The hardest thing you will do today is to listen, not just hear, but to listen. You can hear something and still not listen to it. People do it all the time. To listen is to pay attention. God is speaking right now, but we must slow down and listen to Him. John 5:24

Lord's Supper

When someone says, "I forgot," he is actually saying, "I don't care." No one forgets his own birthday, his graduation, or payday. We remember what's important to us. Jesus said, "Do this in remembrance of me." He wanted the church to always remember the sacrifice He made to bring us salvation. Our redemption didn't come from K-Mart on a blue-light special or from Family Dollar on the half-off sale. It cost the Lord His life. When we take communion, let's repent, refocus, and rededicate ourselves to our assignments. 1 Corinthians 11:23-30

Love

When we see a handsome man with a not so beautiful woman or vice versa, we think, what in the world is that good-looking man doing with that ugly woman? Advice: Stay out of those folks' business. You can't see what he sees in her; he loves her in spite of how she looks. A truly odd couple is Christ and His Church. We're mean, implacable, obnoxious, uncaring, unlovely, and hard to manage, but He loves us in spite of us. He sees something in us we can't see in ourselves. I am so glad the Lord doesn't love us because we're beautiful. We're beautiful because He loves us. Ephesians 5:25-27

"Above all, love each other deeply because love covers a multitude of sins." 1 Peter 4:8. Most of us don't realize when we're being played. As Percy Sledge said, "loving eyes can never see." When you love someone, you have a tendency to overlook his/her faults and only see the positive. Payback to players comes in double portions especially if a Christian is involved. God is not mocked. Whatever people sow, that shall they reap. If you take advantage of someone's heart, know this—it's coming back to you.

Co-dependency is not love. Just because someone completes your sentences, holds your hand in public, and gives you a warm and fuzzy feeling in your stomach when you're together, it doesn't mean it is love. True love is a willingness to sacrifice/suffer on behalf of another expecting nothing in return. This is biblical love, agape, which was on display at Calvary. If Jesus loved us enough to die on our behalf, at least, we should love Him enough to live for Him. John 3:16

The verse says, "God so loved the world that He gave His only begotten Son." It didn't say He so loved the saints. It didn't say He so loved the church, the righteous, the pure, or the good and holy, but the world. God gave His Son for sinners like you and me! If God loved us enough to give His Son for filthy sinners like us, why can't we love the unsaved? When you see someone who is not saved, demonstrate love. After all, it's what God did for you. John 3:16

Do you want your man to love you to life, lose his breath when you walk by, have palpitations when your name is mentioned and never have a desire to cheat on you? Believe it or not it's easy to get him to do these things, but many women have bought the proverbial hype that they have to challenge a man in order to get respect. The answer is in one word—submission. The Lord expects the Church to submit to Him, and He requires wives to submit to their husbands. In return, the husband will love her enough to die for her, that's a fact!

There is one condition. Make sure He is a godly man. You can't make a race horse out of a mule. Ephesians 5:22-33

We must love some people from a distance. If you keep sticking your hand in a fire and expecting a different result, it's not the fire's fault. Church is the best thing God has on the planet, but many of us have been emotionally lacerated by church folk. There's no hurt like "church hurt." The very place we go for comfort and peace is where the enemy wants to inhabit and position his helpers. Don't be discouraged from worship by mean people. It's just the devil's attempt to rob you of your joy and completeness in Christ. Keep loving but keep your distance. Ephesians 6:10-17

I saw a guy with a ball cap with the inscription, "I love Jesus" written on it. Now I know and respect his sentiment for witnessing, but shouldn't the emphasis be on Christ's love for us rather than our love for Christ? Sometimes, I don't love the Lord like I should. When someone cuts me off in traffic, tells a lie on me, keys my truck for no reason, or breaks into my house, I have difficulty walking in love. Sometimes I get angry and act like I don't love Jesus, but, in spite of my inconsistent behavior, Jesus still loves me! You can say mean things about people and others will shun them, but there's nothing anyone can say or do to make Jesus love you less. Oh, how Jesus loves us. John 3:16

The only person who grieves is the person who risks loving. If you live long enough, you will be hurt, but don't let that pain define your future. Keep loving and believing in God. He gives us the capacity to love, and when we are hurt, it is an indication we are being obedient to His Word. Don't spend time hating the person who deceived you in that relationship. There is a balm in Gilead. His name is Jesus. Forget it! Open your heart and make yourself available to love again. That's what life is all about. Jeremiah 8:21, 22

If you want to know if someone loves you, it's not in her kiss, her voice, or her eyes. It's in her giving. You can give without loving, but it is impossible to love without giving. If someone is constantly making demands of you—money, sex, invasion of privacy (wants to know where you are all the time), the person doesn't love you. Love has your best interest at heart and actually enjoys seeing you smile. God is love and everything He created gives back to the world, but His greatest gift was His Son at Calvary. Receive this gift today. He loves you. John 3:16

Don't mistake correction for "hating." If I love you, I have a duty to warn you of pending danger. True love corrects gently to restore. It's not what's said but the attitude and motivation behind what's said. If you see people you love headed in the wrong direction, please warn them, but choose your words wisely. If you are being reproved, listen very carefully. Galatians 6:1

If you love something, let it go. If it loves you, it will come back to you. If it doesn't, you've lost nothing. Stop trying to hold on to someone who wants to get away from you. Life is too short to live in misery. Young lady, if you are making concessions and violating your chastity just to keep a man's attention, you will regret it later. Look in the mirror. You are a creation of God, and He doesn't intend for you to be sacrificed at the altar of someone else's lust. If he doesn't respect your commitment to Christ, he's not the one for you. Proverbs 31:10

Look deeper than the surface. Human behavior is predicated on past experiences with other humans. The cantankerous supervisor, the co-worker who shuns you, a rebellious youth, and the neighbor who won't speak may feel like no one cares for him. That could be the reason for their negative reaction to you. Be the Christian the Bible describes. Engage them in a caring fashion. You may be surprised at what you discover. 1 Corinthians 13

If you told me I was a sinner, you'd be telling the truth, but your attitude would be wrong. It's not enough to tell the truth to win people to Christ; we must also do it in love. There will be an influx of souls entering the Kingdom when Christians learn this because it is our sanctimonious attitude that turns people away. Yes, tell people there is a hell, but don't tell them as if you're glad about it. Let's work on our attitudes. 1 John 1

If someone tells you, "I love you," you're truly blessed. When someone loves you, it is more precious than all the gold in Fort Knox because it connects you to another human spirit. Many of us are under stress every Christmas season trying to buy the latest electronic gadget that's storming the internet or the chic fashions that are promoted as "must- haves" by Madison Avenue. Nevertheless, if you woke up in a home with one person who truly loves you, be thankful. Tell your loved ones you love them; it's a wonderful gift. John 3:16

"People will let you say strong things to them if they know you love them." ~ Haddon Robinson. Love is an essential component of preaching. If you love your congregation, they will accept your rebuke. However, if your motive is self-serving, they will reject it. We need to get back to apostolic preaching which transformed lives across the globe. When you stand Sunday morning, make sure you speak from a place of love. John 3:1

Want to know if someone loves you? Does the person give you their time, talent and treasure? If you're in any kind of relationship, friendship or romantic, and you are always giving and never receiving, the person you're with doesn't love you. Rather, he loves himself and enjoys what you do for him. There is nothing you can do to make anyone love you; they either do or they don't. Save yourself a lot of heartache and sever ties with people who use you for their own advantage. John 3:16

When people walk out of your life, it's senseless to chase them. They left either because they were confused or they wanted to be someplace else. Either way they didn't appreciate your company. Let them go. Concentrate on being the best you that you can be. God has something better for you than what left you.

Three of the most dangerous words in the English language are "I don't care." If we are inhabitants of planet Earth, we should care about what's happening around us—politically, socially, and especially spiritually. Ultimately what happens to one will happen to all of us, so let's pay attention and get involved or we will suffer the consequences.

Jesus wants us to treat everyone fairly, gay, straight, white, black, Jew-Palestinian, and Christian and atheist. Disagreeing with how a person chooses to live his life never warrants hatred and economic discrimination. When we control the means of society and sequester groups that we disagree with, we become reflections of the same thing we dislike about them. Love conquers all. Winning the world entails engaging people with truth and love which can never be done in a vacuum. The gospel is only effective when we preach it with love. Luke 6:31

Falling in love is a risky business because you never know what the other person is going to do with your heart. Sometimes the person you meet says all the right things and appears to be the perfect mate for you, but when you fall for the person, he completely changes. The best thing to do is to follow the instructions of the Bible and never trust anyone with your heart except someone who is committed to the Lord. If the person is devoted to Christ, his principles are in order. Therefore, your feelings will never be played with. The operative words are "devoted to Christ" not in the church. 2 Corinthians 6:14

There is somebody somewhere for everybody, but sometimes we must be patient until we find the person or they find us. If you are without a sweetheart on Valentine's Day, put your arms around your chest and give yourself a big hug. Then tell yourself, "God loves me." Happy Valentine's Day! John 3:16

When you love people, they can do nothing wrong, but when you don't, they can do nothing right. Love hides a multitude of faults, but resentment finds every flaw. Why do people nitpick? It's because they don't like you which is an indication that you need to give them some space. When you have spinach in your teeth, a friend will tell you, but fault finders will tell everyone but you. Choose the company who magnifies your virtues and minimizes your faults. 1 Peter 4:8

Luck

Let's just face it. Nothing in this life comes easy. You can't eat your way to being slim. You can't save money by buying a car. It's impossible to feed a child with just "pennies" a day. Buying that lotto ticket according to your dream won't make it hit. Eating black-eyed peas and collards today won't bring dollars and cents this year and feeding the monster of "more" won't make you happy. I don't want to be a party pooper and rain on anyone's parade, but if it seems too good to be true, it probably is not true. God has ordained that in order to receive benefits we must practice discipline and employ extraordinary effort. Let's set some goals this year and work towards achieving them. Genesis 3:17-19

Marriage

To be a queen, you must have a king. There is no such thing as a queen without the existence of a king. Lesson: Sisters you can't claim queenship if you treat your man like a field hand. A real queen honors, respects, and submits to her king. She also loves and adores her king. As a result, her king loves her like his queen. What some of us call a "strong" woman is nothing but a mad woman. Just because you throw you weight around and force your opinions on everyone doesn't make you strong. Remember that real strength is made perfect in weakness. 2 Corinthians 12:9, Ephesians 5:22-33

If you own a car anywhere in America, the proof of it must be written on paper. If you own a house, the same is true. The proof must be on paper. In some states, ownership of a pet must be proven by putting the evidence down in written form. Tell me why a woman would live with a man without a marriage license. Since his love for his car, his house and his dog has been proven in written form, why would she accept him saying that he's not ready to wed? Marriage is still God's standard for the home. Put it on paper. Ephesians 5:25

When men want to play, they go to the club to find women. When they want a soul mate to marry and settle down, they come to church. They know the best women go to church. If you have a wife or a girlfriend who attends church and you don't go with her, don't be surprised if she gets "hit on." There are a lot of roving eyes in the pews. Go to church with your woman; you might see why she enjoys it so much. Psalms 122:1

I was asked if I would marry someone in the church who had been shacking. My response was "Absolutely!" If the couple has repented and want to live for Christ, why shouldn't the church embrace them? The church is a center for restoration. We've got to stop being so dogmatic and sanctimonious. We can't hide behind the Scripture to justify our religious arrogance. We throw out unwed mothers and look away from the guy who impregnated her. Sin is sin, but it can be forgiven. That's the good news! Let's all remember where we were before Christ saved us. Ephesians 1:7

"And said, for this cause shall a man leave father and mother, and shall cleave to his wife: and they twain shall be one flesh? Wherefore they are no more twain, but one flesh. What therefore God hath joined together, let not man put asunder." Matthew 19:5, 6. This is one of the most broken commandments committed by parents with married children. Yes, he's your child, but he is not under your control any longer. Your child belongs to his wife. If you love the Lord like you say you do, obey His Word and stay out of their home and mind your own business. I know it's hard, but we sin when we meddle in our grown children's homes.

Husbands should never act as lords over their wives' bodies and vice versa. Neither the husband nor the wife owns their body; it belongs to the other. When a spouse uses sex as a reward or punishment, he creates the potential for Satan to tempt the other spouse. The devil has destroyed many marriages because couples use sex as a weapon against each other rather than a blessing. Understand this. If you make your bed hard, you have to sleep in it. 1 Corinthians 7:3-5

Every young couple needs to be in a church. It's hard enough to stay together when you are in the church, and it's impossible to have a healthy relationship without the church. Yes, there are hypocrites in the church, and there are money-hungry ministers, but there is no excuse for not seeking out a church where you feel comfortable together. Your children will greatly benefit from seeing you both going to church on Sunday morning. Please, for your children's sake, and for the sake of your relationship, find a church where you can relate to the people and pastor. Go to church. Hebrews 10:25

All forms of gambling are frowned upon today by preachers except marriage. Let's face it. When two people decide to spend the rest of their lives together, they both are taking a risk. It is a biological fact that all of the cells in a human body renew themselves every seven years. This means all of us become new people every seven years, physically, emotionally and spiritually. If husbands and wives don't invest serious effort in their marriages to grow and change together, the marriage won't last. Maintaining a healthy relationship requires hard work. If your marriage is to survive, you will have to work at it. Ephesians 5:33

My grandparents had a wooden poster on their wall for years that made no sense to me as a little boy. It read, "He who argues and fights with his wife all day will get no piece at night." What puzzled me was the use of the word "piece." Today it makes all the sense in the world. Brothers, if you handle the kitchen, living room, den, and bathroom correctly, you won't have any problem in the bedroom. Sex starts when you pay bills, give compliments, change the oil in her car, or cut the lawn. A romantic fire is often kindled by a little spark in the park. Ephesians 5:25

Marriage is a union of a man and a woman not a conglomerate of families. Many divorces occur because parents won't let go of their children. Dad, when you gave your daughter away at her wedding, you did just that. You gave her away. It is difficult, and you will need divine intervention, but you have to stay out of your daughter's marriage. Yes, mom, you carried him for nine months, but he's grown and gone now, let him go. Families should show up at the wedding but stay away from the marriage. Meddling parents do more damage to marriages than financial problems and compatibility combined. Let your kids make their own mistakes like you did. Matthews 19:6

Lots of people got married because they didn't want to spend evenings alone and then got a divorce for the same reason. Don't rush into marriage just because of societal pressure and social image. Make sure the elements of commonality of faith, interests and, yes, physical attraction are present. Then saturate your decision in prayer. Even then, marriage will still be challenging. Don't be fooled by the image you see in your church of "the perfect marriage," there's no such thing. It takes work, and lots of it. Matthews 19:6

Maturity

Trying to communicate with carnal people is like trying to make a race horse out of a jackass. It's like trying to make a clown look presidential. Don't debate the Word with unspiritual people; you're wasting your time. God has hidden these things from them because of their unbelief. They can't see, but He has revealed His truths to babies. Some of them think they're "deep" because of their ability to excite a crowd, but Beyoncé and Jay-Z can do that as well. Only the anointing can destroy yokes. 1 Corinthians 2:10-16

A sign of maturity is when you break from your mentor and form your own opinions. We all have people in our lives we respect and love, but we must understand that we are not them. God made each of us unique, and we have a purpose and an assignment to complete. No one becomes great being a "yes-man/woman." Joshua followed Moses, but he had to leave Moses. Elisha followed Elijah but eventually he had to separate from Elijah. Barnabas followed Paul, but he had to leave Paul. Do your own thing. Jeremiah 1:7-10

We are not called upon to change people but to meet them where they are and accept them. God does the transformation through His Word and Holy Spirit. Anything you can talk someone into, someone else can talk them out of. You can meet people who don't believe that homosexuality, sexual promiscuity, bigamy, and polygamy are wrong. We have to meet them where they are and escort them to where they need to be by putting an example of holiness and love before them. Let's stop trying to clean fish before they are caught. Jeremiah 31:3

Mercy

God is not fair. The word "fair" is a legal term which means you get what you deserve; therefore, I'm glad that God is not fair. God is just. He may not treat us all alike, but He does treat us all justly. The truth is we can't treat all of our kids alike. Some children listen to instructions well, but others have to be carried to the wood shed. Even though God is just, He has one other attribute that overrides His justice. It's called mercy. Had it not been for His mercy, where would we be today? Lamentations 3:22, 23

It is so easy to condemn someone for an indiscretion when we are not guilty of it ourselves. Highlighting the weakness of others seems to be the favorite past time of some people, but let's consider our own struggles before we start pointing fingers. Your weakness may not be mine and mine may not be yours, but all of us have one. God has given each one of us a thorn to keep us humble. Let's show mercy towards each other because sooner or later we will need some. 2 Corinthians 12:1-10

Yes! We have another day to get it right. I know you messed up royally yesterday. You probably spoke harsh words to someone, went back on a promise you made to God, and your moral ship capsized in the sea of self-indulgence. Still, that was yesterday. This day is a gift the Lord gave us to clean up the mess we made. Let's use it to undo the damage we did yesterday. That's what Christianity is all about—another chance. Use it wisely. Lamentations 3:22-23

Mind

Old habits die hard? No, old habits must be killed. A habit is learned behavior. To break it, it must be unlearned. Whenever we do something, an end road is created in the mind. Satan takes that road and begins to set up camp. He has a right to be there because you gave him permission. To remove him, you have to kick him out, close the road, put up blockades and put the Holy Ghost at the gate. Let's kill some bad habits by protecting our minds. Philippians 2:5

A mind is like a parachute; it's no good unless it opens. ~Frank Zappa. Let's learn to listen to the opinions of others before we pass judgment. Because of preconceived notions, we've had wars, denominational divides, divorces, stereotyping, and racial profiling. When you make up your mind before you get all the information, you're going to always be wrong in your assessment. Learning is like climbing a ladder. We must let go of the lower rung and reach to a higher one to move upwards. Some things we believe keep us from moving to the next level. Let's respect everyone's opinion. Romans 12:2

Ministry

All Christians are ministers and many of us don't realize it. If you are saved, you have a ministry in the body of Christ. Many of us desire the spotlight and the stage where all the attention is focused but the most important part of any ministry is unseen. When you see a duck swimming across the pond, she seems to be just sailing along, but if you could see beneath the water, you'd see her little webbed feet working frantically to push her body along. There's more to any church than the pulpit, and God rewards those who do what they do without fanfare. Be faithful to your calling. 1 Corinthians 12:23, 24

When someone is having relational problems, it's so easy to give our opinion as to what needs to done. Telling someone to leave falls from our lips like pollen on spring lilies when we are on the outside looking in. When the shoe is on our foot, it's a totally different story. God allows us go through things so we can empathize rather than criticize people. It is impossible to minister to hurting people without empathy. The only way to relate/identify with the people we are sent to is to suffer with them. There is no ministry without misery. Be careful how you give advice if you haven't "been there." Hebrews 4:15

Struggles are indications that God is not through with us. I'm not gay, but my hat is off to those who are struggling with their sexuality rather than giving in. When the struggle is over, God is finished with us. All of us who are saved are struggling with issues whether we confess it or not. It's just that we have different problems that we struggle with. Therefore, every believer should extend his arms to our brothers or sisters. We must admit that we are all in the same fallen state and need each other to live righteous lives. Let's support one another and pull off these self-assigned halos, then we are truly ready to minister for Christ. 2 Corinthians 12:7-11

A part of us is lost when we disregard those who contributed to our lives. We have made it out of the hood and have learned how to write a check. We went to college and learned how to conjugate a sentence and live roach free. Still, we should always remember where we started. "The same people you meet on your way up the ladder, you're going to pass on your way back down." ~Unknown. Ministry is caring for the less fortunate, the under privileged and "down and out." Title worshipping, material hungry, fame seeking preachers are in for a big fall off their ladders. God loves His Church too much to let humans ruin it. Fear God, love His Church, and honor His Word and you can always go home. Micah: 6:8

Christians are intercessors. When you see an ambulance, start praying. If you pass an accident on the interstate, pray. When you pass a funeral procession, pray for the family. While watching the news, pray for our country, the president, Senate and Congress. Just pray! You don't have to know the people you're praying for. God does, and that's enough, just pray. The greatest prayers you will ever pray are the ones you do in secret. Just pray. Luke 18:1

The sun could not compete with the Son on Good Friday, so it hid in order for Him to shine. If the sun could not out shine Jesus, why do humans think they can? The only light we have is given to us by Him, and apart from Him there's total darkness. Real ministry is humbling self and projecting His light for the world to see Him. Anything else is flesh on parade. Matthew 5:16

Never wrestle with a pig because you will both get dirty, and the pig enjoys it. Trying to get "one up" or even with someone who has lied on you only hurts you. When they lied on Jesus, He never responded. He stayed on course doing the will of the Father. You can't stop people from lying, but you can make sure the things they say are lies. Luke 23:8-10

"The only way to keep a broken vessel full is to keep it under the faucet." ~D.L. Moody. God breaks us to use us, and when He does, it's painful. God wants us close to Him so He can use us. 2 Corinthians 12

The gospel of John places the cleansing of the temple at the beginning of Jesus' ministry, Matthew, Mark and Luke place it just prior to Jesus' crucifixion. Was John mistaken? Or did Jesus see the same thing at the end of His ministry that He saw at the beginning? The latter is true. If you feel like you are not making a difference in your ministry, remember this, if Jesus couldn't straighten the church out, neither can you. Just be faithful in your calling and let God handle the rest. Jesus died for the Church; it makes no sense for you to die for it too. John 2:13-16

"It is only when we forget ourselves that we do something that people remember." ~Unknown. Many of us are trying too hard to be recognized, and we wonder why our ministries are not growing. They will never grow if they are me-centered. God will make sure of it. If you don't have time to greet people on the street or speak to them after your sermon, you shouldn't have preached to them. All of us should take an introspective look at ourselves and ask "why" we are doing ministry. If the answer is anything other than caring about people, we are in the wrong business. John 20:15-17

Telling someone "I know how you feel" is a terrible mistake when comforting or witnessing to them. We really don't know how anyone else feels about losing a loved one or experiencing a dire physical prognosis or diagnosis. People respond to calamity in different ways because of their temperaments and emotional attachments. There are some people who can't handle catastrophes and when we tell them, "I know how you feel," it turns them off. The only one who actually knows how we feel is Jesus. Recommend Him instead of yourself. Hebrews 4:15, 16

I challenge anyone, saved or not, to walk the hallways of a nursing home, cancer ward or hospital to see if your view of life is not altered. If it's not, you don't have a soul. We may be young, strong, and good-looking today, but we are all just a doctor's visit, a medical test, and a few years from the same fate. One day what you saw there is going to be you, so while we have our health and strength, we all ought to do something to help hurting people make their lives a little better. It may be sooner than you think. Ecclesiastes 3

The reason the Apostle Paul was such an effective minister of the gospel was that he was honest about his struggles. Our culture sees ministers as super human, larger than life perfectionists, who have direct lines to the throne of God. Nothing can be further from the truth. Ministers are human. They struggle with sinful inclinations and doubts just like everyone else. Preachers, be transparent in your pulpit and stop projecting the false image of holiness. Your people need to know that you need God like they do. Romans 7

Those who are hungry for praise will never be able to handle criticism because their egos control their actions. If we put our egos in check, no one could ever hurt our feelings. We are hurt by criticism because it insults our ego and we respond in kind. Subdue your ego and it won't matter what people say about how you preached, ministered in song, or made that presentation. Yes, we all need encouragement, but that shouldn't be the goal of our actions. Our main objective should be to please the Lord. If we please Him, it doesn't matter who we displease. If we displease Him, it doesn't matter who we please. James 4:10

Accountability is the key to ministerial integrity. If there is no oversight and no repercussions for being a "loose cannon," many preachers will say and do some absurd things. There are different levels of convictions in ministry, so the weakest of us need to be checked by the strongest. If you see a brother compromising the gospel, rest assured there is no oversight. Therefore, stricter measures need to be in place for ordaining preachers or we will create monsters that portray themselves as preachers. Timothy 5:21, 22

Life is like an overnight bag. If you attempt to cram too much into it, it splits wide open. There are only 24 hours in a day. You are only one person, and you can't minister to everyone you meet. Yes, it is paramount that we reach as many people as we can, but you can't do it all by yourself. Prioritize your day, delegate some things, eliminate others and regulate the rest to suit your abilities. Let no one put items on your agenda that will cost you more than you can pay. "Failure to prepare on your part does not constitute an emergency on mine." ~Unknown. When they've put you in a straitjacket, they will move on to their next victim. Proverbs 20:4

No one survives long in ministry by attempting to stand alone. When you are young, being a charismatic, quick-witted, and sharp thinker will attract hordes of people, but at the end of the day, you are going to need the fellowship with believers to encourage you in the midst of confusion. People who flock to you now are fickle and looking for the sensationalistic presence you provide. This won't last long. Stay attached to a legitimate umbrella of organized believers because you will need them down the road. Mark 3:24

Money

If you do what you do solely for the money, you will never be content with what you are doing. On the other hand, if you have passion for what you're doing, you will excel. Money is a devilish motivator. Passion is given to us by God. What are you passionate about? Whatever it is, pursue it with all you have, and the money will follow. Proverbs 18:16

Music

Church music should glorify God. Songs that are used in the world should not be sung in church just because a few words are changed. Sometimes "baby" is changed to "Jesus" and the choir keeps on singing. I have not always been saved, and I know R&B music when I hear it. I know it's a new day and God is doing a new thing, but He's still old school. God never contradicts Himself; He said you can't put "new wine in old skins." 2 Corinthians 6:17

Don't tell me what blesses me. Years ago, a professor in seminary told us that one liner songs came out of the folk tradition and were not worth devoting class time to, so we passed over them. Songs like "Jesus Is On The Mainline," "I'm Going To Hide Behind The Mountain," "In The Morning When The Dark Clouds Roll Away," and "If Your Soul Is Not Anchored In Jesus" still move me. Don't let anyone limit how God blesses you by telling you what they think is the right way to worship. It's a personal thing between you and the Lord. John 4:24

Opposition

One principle of aerodynamics is that with every action there is a reaction. Simply stated, this means with every push there is a push-back. Never expect change to come easily.

"The Lord said unto my Lord, Sit thou at my right hand, until I make thine enemies thy footstool." Psalm 110:1. I was trying to change a light bulb but couldn't reach the fixture, so I grabbed a footstool. While I was up there, the thought hit me, "This is my enemy who helped me perform my task more efficiently." Rather than being frustrated with your opposition, you should to thank them because they will help you get to the next level. No wonder Jesus said, "Love your enemies." Tell me again why you're upset with haters?

The words opposition and opportunity come from the same root. No one likes criticism, humiliation, or rebuke but think of these things as opportunities rather than opposition. A plane, which weighs 50 tons, would never have gotten off the ground if it was not opposed by the wind. Every time you see a plane in flight, it is because it mounted up on its opposition. Cancel your pity party and embrace your opposition. Isaiah 40:31

If you owned a business and you gave an employee a direct order, what would you do if he hemmed and hawed about doing it? Would you fire him? Well, God has given every one of us assignments. We all were born for a purpose. What do you think God should do when we don't complete our assignment? Let's remember. If we disobey our boss, the most that could happen to us is we get fired, but if we disobey God, He's in charge of breathing. Jeremiah 29:11

Past

The same storm that rocks the ship also moves the ship. We didn't realize when we were in the storm that the Lord sent us into it to get us to the "other side." Many of us wouldn't have the spouse, job, house, peace of mind, etc., if the storm hadn't occurred. Therefore, we should "bless those" of our past who caused the storm because had it not been for them, we wouldn't be who we are today. Habakkuk 3:17-19

If you want to know your future, look in your past. If you want to know what someone is going to do to you, then look at what you've done to someone else. Your past is the best predictor of your future. Therefore, you can plan a great future starting today by being kind to someone who is hurting, giving to someone who's in need, encouraging someone who wants to quit, praying for someone who is unsaved, consoling someone in bereavement, and simply doing to others as you would have them do to you. Galatians 6:7

You have a chance to turn it around. I know you messed up royally. Yes, you fumbled at the one-yard line. Your "so called" friends laughed when they saw your pain and something is telling you to get even. Listen, I have a word to the wise. Forget your past. God has given you another chance. How do I know? You're still alive. If you can read this, you can turn your life around if you want to. You need only do four things:

1. Repent
2. Believe the Word
3. Act on the Word
4. Be consistent.

I'm not promising a trouble-free future but a God accompanied future. If God is for you, who can be against you? This year will be a great year. Philippians 3:13, 14

If your plans for the future include returning to your past, then your future is doomed. It's human to become nostalgic, but don't live there. Never use these phrases, "I used to be, I used to do, there was a time when, the good old days, things ain't like they used to be" Though those things may be true, you have to move on. Nothing hinders church or personal growth more than people who refuse to let go of what "used to be." Learn from and respect the past but stay focused on what tomorrow holds. Keep it moving. Philippians 3:13, 14.

"Don't stumble over something in your past" ~Unknown. There is always the temptation for us to re-create the past by sacrificing our future. The joys and sorrows of our past are over. You can't put toothpaste back into the tube, and you cannot unscramble an egg. There's nothing we can do to change yesterday. What's done is done. However, there is something we can do. We can take the lessons we learned and apply them to our lives. We can endeavor not to repeat our mistakes. Sometimes bad choices can bring us to a good place. Learn from yesterday but keep looking ahead. It's better to gaze at the future than to glance into the past. Philippians 3:13-14

Patience

The word "through" is a preposition. The prefix "pre" means before and "position" means location. Whenever you're going through, you're simply at a position before you reach your ultimate destination. God took the Israelites through the wilderness before He led them into the Promised Land. God always takes us through before He leads us to our destiny. Be patient my friends when you're going through. God is trying to get you to your destiny. Matthew 4:1

Slow down. The highways, malls, interstates and shopping centers are filled with people who are about to blow a gasket with stress, trying to get to the next store only to find out they don't have what they are looking for. Be patient. Enjoy your day; it is a gift from God! Think of it like this. You're buying that gift to show love, right? Why not show love to the person who just cut you off in traffic? Why run a red light when the next one you approach will stop you anyway? Lastly, take some time to minister to yourself. No woodsman wastes time when he stops to sharpen his ax. Put your mask on first. Psalms 118:24

I was preaching in a certain city where there was a beautiful mountain. The host of the revival told me that his 73- year- old father walked up the mountain quite often, so I asked if I could tag along. I started out walking rapidly while the old guy slowly and steadily walked behind me. By the time we were half way up, I was spent. The old guy said, "The key to walking up this mountain is to take your time. If you don't, you won't make it." Many young ministers are trying to get to the top too fast. Consequently, they will burn themselves out. There are no short-cuts or easy paths to successful ministry. It's hard work, sacrifice, emotional, and sometimes physical pain. Young preacher, you can't be a wonder overnight. Take your time and develop your skills. Go to school and get a good education, but most of all learn to respect your elders. God places no one in leadership until they learn "followship." Enjoy the second chariot as long as you can because the scenery changes when you are in the first one. 1 Peter 5:5

Slow down. There's no need to hurry. Tomorrow will come with or without you. Tailgating, cutting others off in traffic, and passing on the yellow line make no sense. The two minutes you save by speeding down the street is not worth your life. Why rush towards the day of your death? Enjoy today because tomorrow is not promised to you. It's better to be patient on the road than to be a patient in the hospital. Ecclesiastes 7:8

Sometimes it's harder to wait than to do something. At other times it's harder to do something than to wait. Rest assured that whichever is hardest for you is what God wants you to do. Why? He wants you to trust Him. God makes a promise, faith believes it, hope anticipates it, and patience quietly awaits it. You will never get to your promised land if you don't have patience in your wilderness. Trust God. Romans 5:3

Peace

Do you remember visiting Grandma back in the day when she was sitting in front of the fireplace/ heater with her eyes focused on the fire? There was no radio. She was not reading the newspaper, and

116

there wasn't even a TV playing. The house was so quiet you could hear birds chirping outside. It reeked with the smell of smoke and the pleasant aroma of the pies she had cooked the day before. You probably thought, "This deafening silence is driving me crazy." Do you know why she was so content sitting there by herself with such tranquility? It was because she had done everything you are thinking about doing and discovered that none of it was worth it. She had found peace inside herself. Peace is found on the inside not outside of you. Too bad we have to get old to see this. Ecclesiastes 1:14, 12:13, 14

Perseverance

Insanity is doing the same thing over and over and expecting a different result. In order to achieve a desired goal, a variety of approaches must be taken. Many may fail, but failure is not final. Let's do something different today, even if it's nothing but taking a different route home from work. Variety is the spice of life. Genesis 1:31

You're not a failure until you quit. The greatest tool the enemy has is discouragement. He uses it well but he doesn't know it's working unless it registers in your behavior or body language. You are not a defeated Christian. Put a smile on your face, be kind to people, and keep praising the Lord even when you don't feel like it. Let's confuse the hell out of the devil. When he has delivered his best blow, smile and say, "Hallelujah!" Galatians 6:9

A pearl is formed when a grain of sand or foreign object enters into the mollusk of an oyster and causes an irritation. To soothe the pain of the irritation, nectar is secreted around the object and eventually hardens thus creating a beautiful gem. What's irritating you today? Whatever it is, God allowed it. It is not for your demise but to produce jewels for the world to see. From our struggles come our strength and beauty. Hang in there. Endure hardness and when the trial is over, you'll come forth as a pearl of a great price. Matthew 13:45, 46

It is always darkest just before daylight. Pain is always more intense just before deliverance and your greatest attack will come before your breakthrough. If you can make it one more day, just one, you will be closer to God's goal for your life. Don't quit. If you are under severe attack, know this—you are on to something. Satan doesn't focus his energy on conquered ground but that which threatens him. We ought to live so that when our feet hit the floor in the morning, the devil's pulse rises. Stay on point! Psalms 30:5

Things that cause some people to break down and others to break up will cause many to break through. Nowhere in the Bible are we promised an easy life. As a matter of fact, it's just the opposite. Remember there will always be opposition before opportunities, misery before a miracle, and setbacks before your breakthrough. Let's take our eyes off our circumstances and focus them on our God. He's bigger than any problem we have. Psalms 34:19

You can't quit! Don't even think about it. This life is tough. Challenges face us and there will be more after this one, but don't give up. What if Jesus had quit at Calvary? We would all be lost. Instead, He endured for us. If He didn't quit because of us, we can't quit because of Him. Go back to that pulpit; get back on that choir; go back and speak to the one that insulted you; get back in that class; get off the ground; dust yourself off; repent and get back in the game. The devil hates it when we come back! Don't quit! 2 Timothy 2:3

Perspective

Why "out" the people who didn't show up at your party? Just celebrate with the ones who did.

It's called perspective. If you are on top of a building, you can see a lot further than someone on the ground, but unless you're willing to move, you will continue to have the same vantage point. The same applies with perspective about life. Some people saw Martin Luther King as a rabble rouser; others saw him as a reformer. Some people saw Ronald Reagan as a political genius; yet, others saw him as an elitist. Some people see Donald Trump as a self-serving megalomaniac; others see him as the hope of America. To improve our perspective, we must be willing to move and view all things from another angle. If you are not willing to move, you will always have a skewed perception. Take time to communicate with the people with whom you disagree.

Politics

Somebody has to be the adult in the room. Baltimore was on fire because of extremes, questionable police practices, and camera hogs. In every community there is a sleeping giant of violence and crime looking for an excuse to be awakened. When protests are made, it should be done with civility, calmness, and peace. It was sad to see ministers throwing gasoline on a smoldering fire and disappearing into their comfortable homes to watch the deflagration. We should all take a cue from Dr. Martin Luther King and preach against injustice but take a stand for peace. Preachers, let's remember to be scriptural in everything we say because there are some people who actually listen to what we say. Matthew 5:9

We can't legislate morality. Jesus never commissioned the disciples to go and impose their beliefs on the world; He gave them instructions to preach. It's sad to see so many Christians being misled by self-serving, non-believing politicians who use the public sector as evidence that the church is losing its fight against sin. Sinners will do what sinners do, end of story. Taking away their guns, sexual promiscuity, drugs, and gambling casinos will only open doors for them to sin differently. Yes, we need laws and law enforcement, but that's the government's responsibility. Preachers, let's spend more time on our knees and in the Word of God and less time campaigning for candidates who won't know our names after the election.

Have you ever wondered why Jesus never got involved in politics? Perhaps He knew that a person's political opinion will never change through debating. We waste time arguing with each other about politics because our attitudes aren't shaped by reason but by our emotions. Since our emotions are the shallowest part of us, Jesus chose to target the heart of man to affect change. When the heart changes, the person changes. Preachers, let's do more preaching and less debating. 2 Timothy 4:2

Praise

Accepting criticism as well as praise is a part of the Christian walk. When someone pays us a compliment, let's not let it go to our heads because the next day there will be accusations. Moses went from hero to zero in three days. They praised him at the Rea Sea and complained in the wilderness. When Jesus entered Jerusalem, He was praised. Three days later, they said, "Crucify Him." Let's give God the glory when we are praised. Psalms 33:1

I can't get the image out of my mind of a young woman I saw in Walmart. She was paralyzed on one side of her body because of a stroke; yet, she had the most beautiful smile on her face I have ever seen. Then it hit me. Some saints have a "because of praise" while others have an "in spite of praise." All healthy Christians will praise the Lord because He's been good to us, but how many of us will praise Him in spite of what we're going through in life. When we understand how undeserving we are and how merciful He has been, our souls should leap for joy. Stop looking at the circumstances and praise God in spite of them. Psalms 34:1-3

Praise God! The enemy designed opposition to send you to the psychiatric ward or graveyard but it only shaped your character and drew you closer to God! Praise God again because just looking at you, you don't even look like you went through it! Let no one hold you hostage to your history. Yesterday is gone and tomorrow may never be ours, so we only have Jesus and today but come to think of it, that's all we need! Hug a hater today. They made it ALL possible. Genesis 50:20

Sometimes you don't feel like praising God; praise Him anyway. Sometimes you don't feel like praying; pray anyway. Sometimes you don't feel like forgiving, forgive anyway. Sometimes you don't feel like giving, give anyway. Often you don't feel like being nice to others who've wronged you, be nice anyway. Our feelings shouldn't control our actions, but ultimately, our actions will control our feelings. The quintessential sign of maturity is doing what's necessary even when you don't feel like it. After all, Jesus didn't feel like dying for us, but He did it anyway. Matthew 26:39

Let's be real, praising God is the hardest thing in the world to do, and it looks so stupid to the natural man. The worship leader says "Raise your hands" and our hands get so heavy. The world sees us and laughs at us dancing, singing and clapping to loud music. The same activity goes on in the club, and at the stadium, but no one seems to mind. It's because our deliverance is in our praise and the enemy wants us bound. In every account of victory in the Bible, God ordered the people to praise Him first. Don't wait until the battle is over. Shout now! Joshua 6:1-5

Never criticize anyone's praise because you don't know their story. Why are praise and shouting annoying/funny to the unbeliever? It is because they have not experienced the freedom of forgiveness. When we have been forgiven, the joy of the Lord floods our soul in a way that can only be expressed in ecstatic praise. The more we're forgiven, the greater the praise and the deeper the worship. You don't know like I know what the Lord has done for me. Want a real blessing today? Praise Him. Luke 7:36-50

You make fun of my praise? Go ahead; you just don't understand. If you knew what God has done for me, you wouldn't laugh. You would be shouting too. I hear people say, "I don't know why they are shouting so much with the way they are living." The question isn't why they are shouting so much with the way they are living. The question is why aren't you shouting if you're living so well? God deserves, demands, and desires our gratitude in the form of praise. Let's stop just talking Christianity on Facebook and actually go to church on Sunday. Psalms 107

Until you know people's entire stories, don't judge their praise. Unless you've walked in others' shoes, felt their pain, lived in their neighborhood and experienced their frustrations, you wouldn't understand. Some people think it "doesn't take all that" because they haven't gone through what others have endured. But when you look back and see where you were and then look at where the Lord has brought you, it makes no difference what others think. It is impossible to be dignified after you've been delivered; sometimes praise just comes from nowhere. If the Lord has been good to you, PRAISE HIM. Stop worrying about what people think. Mark 10:46-52

Prayer

In the natural, we wouldn't rebuke a blind man when he tells us he can't see. Why, then, do we argue with someone who tells us that he can't see something in the spiritual world? We learn some things with time. Other things we learn through experience, but some things are only seen through revelation. Before we go about the business of dispensing the gospel, let's spend more time on our knees praying that God will open the eyes of those we are witnessing to. We are not called to talk people into the Kingdom. Anything we talk someone into, someone else can talk them out of. Pray before ministering. 2 Kings 6:17

Where there is light, there is a burning, where there is a burning, there is depletion, where there is depletion, there is death. If we don't refill the fuel for our lights, we die. The filling station is quiet time with God. Have you prayed today? Have you plugged into the fuel pump and refilled your tank? If we don't spend time daily with God, we become weaker and eventually we become ineffective. If you are too busy to pray, you're too busy. Matthew 5:16

When a newborn cries, his mother rushes to him, picks him up, and cuddles him to assuage the pain or problem. When a toddler cries, she walks in caresses him, speaks gently to him, and calms it down. When a six-year-old cries, sometimes it appears that she ignores him to teach the child that life hurts and he must toughen up. If it seems like God is hesitating with an answer to your prayer, it may be He is trying to teach you a lesson about life. We've attempted to make God our servant, when it's the other way around. He's not a bus boy or a bell hop; He's God. He hears you, but He wants you to trust and wait. Isaiah 30:18

When you pray today please remember to thank God for hospital employees, medical assistants and nurses. Sometimes we overlook people who are invaluable to our lives. You will never know a person's worth until you really need him. My hat is off to the staff at Greenwood Hospital for caring for my 87-year-old dad as if he was their own. You are appreciated. 1 Corinthians 13

It's possible to spend too much time rehearsing, singing, teaching, preaching, practicing, preparing to minister and too little time in the presence of God. Many of us are simply over-worked and on the verge of burn-out because we don't seek renewal in our private devotion.

Don't be a ministerial workaholic; sit still today and let God talk to you. None of us wants to be in a one-sided conversation where one person is doing all the talking, and neither does God. Go to your prayer closet and listen. 1 Kings 19:12

Do we really know what we're eating? Many of us eat out every day not knowing if the server washed his hands. We never see the condition of the kitchen and we don't bother to read the restaurant's rating. Most of the food is processed and left from days before. Some of it contains carcinogens, bacteria, and other micro-organisms. The food is high in fat and carbs, not to mention the fact that it has little or no taste. Yet, many of us sit down and ingest this stuff without praying. Shame on us! Dare we put this poison in the temple without consecrating it first? Pray over your food. If you are in such hurry for "fast food" that you don't have time to pray, you're in too big of a hurry. 1 Timothy 4:4, 5

"I'd rather teach ten men to pray than one to preach" ~Charles Spurgeon. Praying is harder than preaching. Someone asked me if I am ever afraid when I stand up to preach? My response was, "Yes, not of the people, but God." God forbids any messenger to go to the pulpit without first communing with the message-giver. It is absolute blasphemy. Preachers, let's talk more to God about what He wants to say to His people. 1 Timothy 2:1, 2

Sometimes life is so draining. It takes all our energy just to make it until tomorrow. Things come after us one behind another and we find ourselves overwhelmed. We don't need a lecture or any kind of advice; sometimes we don't even want to talk. What should we do? At times like these, we need to pray and wait. If you can make it one more day, there's hope in trusting God. He has a plan for all this. Wait on the Lord. Isaiah 40:31

The lion and the gazelle get up each morning with two different perspectives. The lion knows that he has to run faster than the gazelle to catch him, so that he will have dinner. On the other hand, the gazelle knows that he has to run faster than the lion in order to survive. The truth is some mornings we feel like the lion and some mornings we feel like the gazelle. Either way, it is important to begin each day with prayer. This world is a jungle, and we can't make it by ourselves. We all need God's help. Luke 6:12

Just because God is not speaking to you doesn't mean He is not watching you. Sometimes, we feel our prayers are bouncing off the ceiling. That's a good thing because God is not beyond the ceiling. He's beneath the ceiling. He's in your heart. His silence doesn't necessarily mean consent and it does not mean disapproval. He's monitoring your actions to see if you are going to obey His Word in spite of His silence. Listen for His voice, but even when you can't hear Him, trust His Word. Nahum 1:7

Preaching

Whenever clergy are on a balance beam, the efficacy of the gospel will be compromised. Anytime a preacher has to report to a group or an overseer for something they said in the pulpit, that ministry will be ineffective. A preacher who stands to deliver the gospel should have no friends to reward and no enemies to punish. No pastor is free if he is afraid to speak the truth because of the threat of termination. Pastor, if you are in a pulpit where you are being censured, rest assured God will not bless your ministry. Speak the truth. 2 John 1:2

The most hated creature on planet Earth is the black preacher. He is viewed as a rabble rouser, an instigator, and trouble maker. He is the victim of glowing hatred and has been called all kinds of names. Comedians, politicians, and even some of his own parishioners mock him for "eating chicken, driving old Cadillacs, and hacking during his sermons." Yet where would we be without Martin Luther King, Richard Allen, Andrew Young, Fred Shuttlesworth, Wyatt T. Walker, Joseph Lowery, and Jesse Jackson? Yes, there are "shysters" in every profession, but never throw out the baby with the bathwater. Almost every advancement African Americans have received since the abolition of slavery was initiated by black preachers. Never forget the ship that brought you over. Romans 10

How many preachers have said, "I should have studied more, prepared better, prayed harder" in the middle of a sermon. How many times have you felt like you flunked, but after you finished, someone got saved or delivered/blessed? You can't judge the effectiveness of the sermon by audience response. Sometimes when people are shouting at you, they aren't listening. Sometimes when they are quiet, they are actually taking it in. Never mistake the celebrative moment in your message as an indication of successful preaching. The Word is alive and has power all by itself. Isaiah 55:11

Preachers, especially novices, never run into the pulpit of any church unless you are invited to come up. You may be licensed by your denomination and ordained, but that doesn't mean your credentials are accepted by everyone. Your anointing will work in or out of the pulpit so you don't necessarily need a stage. More importantly, it's embarrassing and humiliating to be asked to step down. He who lives by the spotlight dies by the spotlight. Luke 14:9-11

Was it what the preacher said that made you shout, "Amen" or how he said it? Some preachers have a way of embellishing the message with the right words which casts more light on us rather than God. Therefore, our audience sees us rather than the God in us. There's nothing wrong with being creative, but let's be careful not to re-create God in our own image when we preach. The messenger should never overshadow the message. John 12:21

Your pastor does not have it all together regardless of what he portrays. Every time he preaches at a funeral, visits a hospital, counsels a disturbed teen, endures caustic criticism, tries to explain why a child died with cancer, it takes something out of him. He loses part of himself. Not too long ago, six pastors committed suicide and people were puzzled. They shouldn't be. Pastors are people too! We have the same problems you have—bad marriages, disobedient children, addictions, bills, tempers, and temptations like everyone else. Let's be real preachers. We need to tell our congregations the truth and maybe we can reach more people in the world. Tell them to pray for you and your family because you are under attack. The only hope for successful ministry is prayer. 1 Thessalonians 5:25

Preachers, never use the pulpit as a rock pile. It is so easy to become distracted by haters that you can prepare a sermon with the person in mind. Consequently, you end up preaching to one person rather than the whole body of Christ. The objective of Satan is to distract and his mission is accomplished when we focus on someone in the pew who has hurt us. If everyone in your church loves you, you aren't doing something right. Some program you initiated, some sermon you preached, or an ego you offended is fodder for hatred. Suck it up and stay on point. Preach the Word and let the text tailor the truth. 2 Timothy 4:1-5

Preachers, if you have never had someone get up and walk out while you are preaching, either you haven't been preaching long or you're not preaching. We are in a day where "ear candy" is popular and expected by audiences. While it should never be our intention to be abrasive, this Word we carry sometimes will offend folk. No one washes their face with a Brillo pad and nobody cleans their greasy pans with Vaseline Intensive Care. The Word will cut and soothe. It's the Holy Spirit who determines which is necessary. Isaiah 55:11

The only opinion that matters is God's. Preachers, if you have never been threatened by someone because of something you said for Christ, just keep preaching. The Word is like a hammer. It will draw people and drive them. Some of them will be driven to do physical/emotional harm to you. Let's stop trying to please our audiences and concentrate on the assignment that God has placed before us—preaching the Word. This is not a glamorous profession; it's a dangerous one that demands rigorous sacrifices and efforts. Church, please pray for preachers; we're under attack like never before. John 16:2

God gives us opportunities to demonstrate the message before delivering it. It seems that whenever I preach a sermon on" trusting God," I'm faced with a situation where I have to trust Him myself. If I preach on "giving" I am confronted with an opportunity to give. Practice what you preach. You better believe it; God will make sure of it. Hosea 1-3

The Gospel still works. Don't be discouraged because you've been preaching for weeks, months, or years and it seems like people are getting worse. Keep preaching anyway. A homeless man was playing a saxophone on the street while people were walking down the street. Some were dropping money in his cup and others were ignoring him. They all heard the music, but only a few responded. If you preach and 20 get saved, you can't take the credit. If you preach and no one seems to care, you shouldn't take the blame. Just keep preaching anyway. God is in charge of the response. Romans 1:16

Refuse doom and gloom preaching; it's not biblical. In spite of the fact that we are under attack by radical Muslim groups and many churches have grown cold, there is a truth that should bring consolation. The slain Lamb in the beginning of the Book of Revelation rules from the throne at the end of the book as the Lion of the Tribe of Judah. The world is not "going to hell in a hand basket," it's coming to Jesus. When Jesus takes His world back, the Church will inherit it also! Take all the sad-sack preaching and teaching back to hell where it belongs. The Church has hope. Revelations 22

Let them alone. If a pastor doesn't deliver his sermon like you are accustomed, if a church doesn't worship in the fashion you like, if the design of a ministry building puzzles you, if people's dress and appearance offend you, it doesn't mean God isn't using them. Don't set your mouth against any believer who names Christ as Lord. Our biases and preconceived ideas should never dominate our opinions about how ministry should be done. There are no specific instructions in Scripture as to the "right way" to do church, only that it should be done in spirit and truth. No church has a monopoly on worship. Leave them alone and let them do it the way God gave it to them. There are enough devils out here to fight; jump on them. Luke 9:48-50

There's a difference between "feelgoodism" preaching and gospel preaching. One is like a photograph; the other is like a mirror. A photograph can be photo-shopped by adding light and angles to make you look your best. We put our best pictures as profiles on FB, but we don't look like that all the time. A mirror never lies. What you see is the way it is. The objective of "feelgoodism" is to make you feel good even in your sins. The truth is like a mirror that reflects the true you. Don't expect your pastor to preach shouting messages every Sunday. Some sermons will make you sit back and shut up if it's the true Gospel. James 1:22-27

What happens if preachers don't speak the truth? Evil advances. Injustice prevails, and people are lost. Don't be afraid to be controversial and divisive because that's what the Word does. It separates right from wrong. We should turn our ordination papers in if we can stand by and watch teenagers get shot down in the street, observe deception in government, see destruction of biblical families and legislate government sanctioned killing of the unborn. If preachers don't say something about evil, what good are we? God called us to the rocky road of suffering for truth's sake, not the easy street self-service. Preach. 1 Corinthians 9:16

Preachers, let's be very cautious using terms of endearment when referring to women in church. Although you may innocently say, "Honey, Sweetheart, or Sweetie," her husband or boyfriend may not view it as such. He is likely already suspicious of you when he walks in the door because of how preachers are portrayed in the movies, TV, and social media, so let's not give him a reason to shut his ears to our message. The term "sister" works just fine; let's use it. Romans 14:16

Preachers we are not worth our suit and tie if we won't tell the truth. We are good at identifying the problem, but poor at recognizing the solution. A sermon without application is just fussing. The truth involves both identification and application which improve the congregation. God never sends a message without hope. Let's tell the whole truth. Tell them what they are doing wrong but show them how to get it right. 2 Timothy 3:16

If any church is searching for a pastor, the paramount concern should not be what school he attended or whether he's married. Neither should the emphasis be placed on his talents and gifts. The most important thing in selecting a pastor is whether he has sat under authority for a sufficient length of time. If you put a person in leadership who has never followed a good leader, you're going to have a mess on your hands. God made sure that every leader He chose was prepared by forcing him to submit to another human authority. The problem today is that we have too many self-centered, loose cannons in the pulpit. If a deacon, elder, steward, search committee member is reading this, examine a candidate's "followship" before making your selection. 1 Timothy 2:1-7

Misery is drinking a bottle of Smart Water and then going on to the pulpit with a guest evangelist who can't find the landing strip.

Just because a person preaches from the Bible doesn't make his message biblical. The central thread that runs through the scriptures is redemption, and it is summed up in the message of the cross. The

Bible is not a cafeteria where you can pick and choose what you want. It is a prepared meal served by the Holy Spirit. Preachers stick with the text. If you do you will preach Jesus every time. Acts 11:19-21

"Every sermon should give you homework." ~ Dr. Mack King Carter. If you heard a sermon last Sunday and were not challenged to live better, treat people with more kindness, and draw closer to the Lord, you didn't hear the Word. We love to be validated in our wrong, encouraged to stay the course in error, and confirmed in our prejudices. However, the Word always corrects us and points us to Christ. Learn the difference between being spiritually nourished by the Word and cheerleading the flesh. Hebrews 4:12

Preaching without Christ is just philosophy, ideological opinions, and a futile attempt at crowd control. There are so many start-up churches being established, but so few of them are preaching Christ. Preachers, we should re-examine our message to make sure Jesus is the only subject matter in it. Paying tribute to God in a sermon is not gospel preaching, "No man comes to the Father except they come through me." ~John14:6. Thousands of "sermons" will be delivered this Sunday, and the name of Jesus will never be mentioned. Sadder still, many churches will not have an invitation to discipleship. Let's not become victims of cultural pressure to be politically correct by not offending audiences. Preach the Word! 1 Corinthians 9:16

Young preachers: Never walk onto another church's pulpit uninvited. The most embarrassing thing for a novice is to be told to leave the dais and go back to the audience. I pastored a church where I allowed female preachers onto the pulpit, but I left there when I was called to another church. The former church asked me to return to do a revival and I gladly accepted. On the first night, a lady walked up and sat down. The current pastor of that church walked over to her and told her that he was the pastor, so had to step down. She was humiliated and so was I. Learn this. It's not about seats, it's about service. Luke 14:9-11

"Hollering ain't preaching, but there is some hollering in preaching." ~ Dr. Cecil W. Clark. Your mom wouldn't have yelled at you if she was not passionate about you growing up to be a better person. Your coach would not have raised his voice at you if he was not passionate about following orders that protect you in the big game. Passion causes all of us to become emotional. How can anyone be casual and nonchalant about something as important as soul-winning? Preachers, never be embarrassed when you become emotional delivering a sermon, you have a right to. Isaiah 58:1

"When the person on the front row of your church gets tired of hearing you say something, the person of the back row is just getting it." ~James Emery White. In an attempt to be "fresh" every Sunday, many preachers cover material once then we move on to something else. Don't assume people get it the first time; say it again. This goes for parents, supervisors, and teachers as well. It is not always a sign of laziness to be repetitious. Sometimes it is just common sense. Besides, why move on to something else when they are not applying the last thing you said? 1 Timothy 4:6

One dimensional preaching will produce a one-dimensional church. The Bible offers prosperity, fulfilled relationships, supernatural gifts, rewards for faithful stewardship, and the anointing of the Spirit, but there's more than these in Scripture. God never sends anyone to harp on one thing. Some congregations know what their pastor is going to say every time he stands because it's the same sermon with a different text. Christians need to know not only that they are saved, but how they are saved. Teach doctrine rather than components of the gospel. Stop cherry picking: tell it all. 2 Timothy 2:15

There isn't a preacher alive who has not borrowed an idea or two in his sermon preparation. It's okay to borrow, but don't steal. Give credit to your sources; it's the right thing to do. God expects us to labor over a text until it becomes a part of us so that when we stand to declare the Word, we can do it with clarity and passion. Use the ideas of others but make the sermon yours. It will be much more effective. Exodus 20:15

If you hate controversy, you're not called to preach. If you love controversy, you're not called to preach. Controversy is a reality of preaching because preaching goes against the grain of this world. We should expect a head wind in our ministries if we preach the Word. Like a plane needs opposition to fly, we need controversy to transform lives. We are not alone. We have heavenly help. Deliver the message. The message-giver will handle the controversy. Matthew 28:19, 20

Bishop Paul S. Morton established the position of armor bearer in his church because he serves New Orleans, a high crime area where it is possible to be robbed or killed for profit. For some megachurch pastors it is wise to employ body guards to protect life and limb, but if you have 20 members, why do you need armor bearers? You're surrounded at church on Sunday by armor bearers, but Monday morning you are at Walmart by yourself. It appears that you want to project the image of an alpha male to your congregation which is antithetical to New Testament teachings. The world doesn't need any more shows. John 1:23

What's that silence I hear? Where was the outcry from national pastors, evangelists, and church leaders against the tragedy in Orlando? The truth is that many Christians believed the evil perpetration on innocent people was an act of God. Was the Mother Emmanuel shooting an act of God? No. If we don't condemn evil in every form, we are complicit with men and women who believe their assumption of what's right or wrong is the standard. Let's call a spade what it is or we'll pay the consequences. Romans 2:1-4

Preachers, let's use our pulpits to unite people not ignite them. We must have a cool head and a warm heart to make it through these tumultuous days. Moses saw an Egyptian beating a Hebrew, and then he killed the Egyptian. As a result, God's purpose was delayed for forty years. It is not a time to be controlled by anger, but godly wisdom found in the Word of God. If we are people of faith, this, too, will work out for our good and God's glory. Let's give people hope in the midst of mass confusion. Preach only the Word of God. Colossians 1:17

Things I have learned: It is impossible to be a good pastor and have everyone like you. Pastors, we are not in a popularity contest, so we should never expect the key to the city. No matter what we do, someone will criticize and even castigate us. Why not just please God and let the chips fall where they may?

The truth is often rejected because it's spoken in the wrong spirit. All effective ministry incorporates both truth and love. People will only receive truth if the attitude of the person delivering the message has no dog in the fight. If pride, money, fame, and competition motivate the preaching, the message will be regurgitated.

When UPS delivers a package to you, a signature is often required to indicate that the package has been received. When God sends you a word through the sermon, He expects you to sign for it with obedience. Your compliance indicates that the message has been received. Isn't it interesting that we enjoy messages that illuminate the sins of others, but we get mad with the preacher when he comes down our street? Your pastor is nothing but a UPS man. He didn't create the message; he simply delivered it. If you really appreciate your pastor, don't give him a card, give him your obedience. 1 Timothy 5:17

Preachers must be careful how we use the Word against people in our congregations. Some of us use it as a policeman uses a night stick to punish people who have opposed us. When people have fought with the world, their flesh, and the devil all week, they don't need to come to church and get another beating because the pastor is venting personal frustrations. Of course, we must preach against sin, but we must remember truth is only accepted when it is given in a loving spirit. John 21:15-25

All of us are good at identifying problems, but few of us are good at finding solutions. Would you continue to go to a doctor who only diagnosed your illness and never wrote a prescription? Preach the Word and reveal my sin but tell me what to do next. Please tell me what to do to get well rather than explaining to me how ill I am. I know I'm sick because I feel the pain. God never sends the church a message without hope. Romans 15:4

The term "street preaching" was coined by church folk. It's called street preaching because it is not palatable to the sensitive, cultured, and socially conditioned ears of the organized contemporary church. But as Christians we should love the truth regardless of who speaks it. I was converted to Christ by a street preacher. Does it really matter if the preacher's subjects and verbs don't agree? Is it important that the one who's delivering the message have a seminary degree? We are losing millennials by the millions because we have elevated our ecclesiastical traditions over the truth. The truth is the truth no matter who speaks it. Philippians 1:15-18

I heard an old deacon say years ago that no preacher is worth a hundred and fifty dollars a week. Andrew Luck of the Colts makes 24.6 million a year. Drew Breeze of the Saints makes 24.3 million, and Russell Wilson of the Seahawks earns 21.9 million per year. These guys work hard for what they make and there shouldn't be any hate against them, but their ministry only serves for entertainment. The preacher's worth can't be measured in terms of dollars and cents. What we do has eternal consequences. What they do is temporary. Pay your pastor a decent salary, so he can go watch these guys play too. Romans 10:10-17

It's not just speaking truth but speaking truth in love that brings conviction. Jesus never got angry presenting the gospel unless He was speaking to hardened religious folk and political tyrannical magnates. We will never win the world if we use our Christian platform to insult, humiliate and belittle people. We need to ask ourselves what/who we preach. If we preach Jesus, we preach love, and we can't preach love with a mean spirit. After all, Christians were once homosexuals, liars, fornicators, and adulterers just like the ones we target as incorrigible. We should preach against sin, but we should also love the sinner. Ephesians 4:15

Why is it that preachers have to fake perfection to be considered as legitimate prophets? We have to tell people we had a praying mother or a godly father who made incredible sacrifices to nurture us into the Kingdom. We have to pretend that we have the perfect marriage and an ideal family that should be mimicked by our followers if they hope to enter domestic bliss. Real people know better. We are losing many in our evangelical efforts. God calls imperfect people to preach to an imperfect world about the prefect man of salvation. Simply tell them that. After all, it's not about us, it's about Him. 1 Timothy 1:15

If God called you to preach, don't let anyone discourage you from preaching. When people come up to you and tell you they didn't enjoy your sermon, just smile and walk away. Preaching is not to be enjoyed, it is to be obeyed. The devil wants to destroy your enthusiasm for preaching and he will use whatever he can to discourage you. Even when the phone doesn't ring and no one is giving you accolades for your ministry, don't be discouraged. Keep preaching. 2 Timothy 4

Can you imagine this conversation?
Pastor: Apostle Paul, are you available to come preach for us on April 16th-18th?

Apostle Paul: As a matter of fact, I am. There's an opening on my calendar on those dates.

Pastor: Great! We will make sure you are well compensated for your service to us. Thank you so much!

Apostle Paul: Okay, I will have my secretary fax my contract for services rendered.

Pastor: Contract?

Apostle Paul: Yes, my fee is $1000 dollars a night, a first-class airline ticket, a five-star hotel, and a limo to bring me to church each night. I also require Evian water in the pulpit, hot tea in the study, and room service at my hotel.

Pastor: But we are not financially capable to provide all that, sir.

Apostle Paul: Well, I'm sorry, I can't come to you.

Pastor: But you said, "Woe unto me if I preach not the gospel of Christ." Shall I remind you that you also said "of necessity I preach the gospel?" And Jesus our Lord said, "Whatever is set before you receive it joyfully!"

Apostle Paul: Well, that was back in the first century. Things have changed. I have to charge because people will take advantage of me.

Pastor: Thanks for your time Apostle, but we can't afford that cost. We will have to call someone else.

"My pastor won't let me have a trial sermon!" How many times we've heard this from someone itching to get onto the pulpit. If you are called of God, no one can prevent you from preaching but yourself. Preaching is not something you do, it's who you are, and you don't need permission from man to do what God has called you to do. Start preaching to your best friend, your family, and then your neighborhood. When your pastor sees that you are a preacher, he will give you an opportunity to come to the stage. Your problem may be that you want the stage rather than souls. 1 Timothy 3

Simply downloading data to a congregation is not preaching. They can get information from the internet. Preaching has to be informative, but more than that, it has to be inspirational. And only the Holy Spirit can inspire people to come to Jesus, live holier lives, and love one another. Preachers, let's spend more time on our knees before the Lord than in our commentaries. Matthew 14:23

Pastors, there are some people in your congregation whose main objective is to keep your church small. They are afraid that if new people come in they will lose their control. They try to make sure you do everything. They want you to visit the sick (deacon's job), live in your office (staff's job), keep check on seniors at home (missionary's job), and they even like to see you at every meeting at church. Any pastor who is always available is not worth much when he is available. We are administrators whose responsibility is to equip the saints by teaching and preaching the Word. "Do it yourselfers" won't last long in ministry. Even the Lone Ranger had Tonto. Ephesians 4:11, 12

If they are only loyal to you, it won't last long because you are going to say or do something that's going to upset them. If they are loyal to God, they will overlook your imperfections because they know that you are a human like everyone else. Put no trust in people who only want to hear you preach and think that you are the epitome of gospel preaching and teaching. Both of you will eventually be sadly disappointed. "Flattery is the food for fools." ~ Unknown.
Psalms 146:2-4

If your dentist retires, you don't let your teeth decay and fall out. You find another dentist. If your doctor dies, you don't stop getting check-ups every year. You find another doctor. Why is it then, that so many people stop going to church when their preacher falls away from the faith into sin? We have heard "All preachers are just alike." If you are looking for an excuse not to go to church, don't blame all preachers. There really aren't enough crutches in the world for all the lame excuses we make for not going to church. Luke 14:18

Did you choose your pastor or did he choose you? However, you answered this question, you are wrong. We don't choose our pastors and our pastors don't choose us, God does the choosing. If you are in a church just because it's your "family church," you're in the wrong church. You leave Sunday morning miserable and spiritually drained, and you're out of place. People are just like plants, they can only grow in the right soil. Sometimes the church votes right after prayer and chooses the right leader, and sometimes the bishop gets it right, but many times this doesn't happen and the whole church suffers. Don't hinder your walk with God by attending a church where you're not being spiritually nurtured. Jeremiah 3:14-16

Prophets speak truth to power, and at no time in history has power dictated to the prophets. Many people in the pulpit have livelihoods that are solely dependent on our preaching. Some of us avoid certain subjects because we know we will be censured. Some of us lost a "good church" because we let the powers that be control what the Holy Spirit was saying to us. Don't be ashamed. Keep preaching. When we meet Jesus, we will not have to answer to our denominations, our bishops, or our elders; we will have to answer to God. Respect your overseers and give deference to your covering but never let men control your ministry. Be sensitive to the Spirit. Only He knows how to do ministry. 1 Timothy 2:7

Gimmicks won't work for long in anything, especially not in ministry. We must stay with proven methods of winning people to the Kingdom and avoid the latest techniques designed by the most popular author/preacher. What really works is sincere, uncompromising, expository preaching. Some will come when you compromise the music of the church, hand out monetary gifts to the one the "Holy Spirit" has declared, or give away a grand prize for the most faithful attendee, but this only swells the church. There is a difference between growing and swelling. When something swells, it will eventually shrink, but growth is permanent. Only the Word of God will grow a congregation to maturity. Preach the Word. Hebrews 5:13

There is something you need to know about your pastor. He has some secrets that he would never share from the pulpit. He also has a past that he is not proud of, but it is his past that produces his passion in preaching. In spite of this, God set him over you to give you His Word of life, and He expects you to obey it. Don't look at your pastor as an icon of perfection. He struggles, probably more than you, and he needs your prayers. No God-sent pastor wants you to put him on a pedestal. He would be satisfied if you would just only be attentive and obedient to the truth. This is reward enough for him. Love, honor, and support him and pay him a decent salary, but never let him eclipse God in your life. Acts 14:8-18

"I'm with you in spirit pastor but I won't be there Sunday." How many preachers have heard this as an excuse for absenteeism from services? You don't send your spirit to pick up your paycheck or go to the dinner table. Why don't people just tell the truth? We go where we want to go and do what we want to do. We should love being in the presence of one another because we are family. If you are a part of a church, be committed to active participation in its programs. The more you give to a church the more you'll love it. I love my church. What about you? Hebrews 10:25

Pride

If you are going to give and boast about it, don't give. If you are going to do something and then complain about it, don't do it. If you are going to go to church to be entertained and critique the service, don't go. God credits attitudes not actions. We look at the what. God looks at the why. Therefore; we often make invalid judgments of each other's intentions. We laugh at the soloist who's singing off key, the preacher who is using poor grammar, and the deacon who is wearing a mismatched suit, but God doesn't care about dress, language or the musical scale. He looks at the heart. Keep your heart pure and let the world laugh. Colossians 3:23

Remember The Wizard of Oz? There was this little old man standing behind a curtain cranking a machine that produced an image which frightened Dorothy and her group. He was projecting an image of himself that was untrue. This describes a lot of us. We promote ourselves and stand behind Jesus saying, "To God be the glory." The Lord doesn't want to be a part of our flesh parade. He wants us to line up behind Him. Isaiah 42:8

Prosperity

Prosperity has done more damage to the Christian church than adversity. Sure, God prospers us. No Biblicist would argue that, but He also sends us some trouble. Adversity is the only diet that will reduce a fat head. God knows that we learn some things from prosperity, but we learn much more through adversity. Learn not to hate the struggle. It is often the means God uses to improve our character. Your character is what you have left when you've lost everything else. Matthew 6:34

Racism

Racism is sin. It cannot be cured by education, legislation, or salvation. The most prevalent establishment in the world is the Church, and it is infested with racism. Many preachers are afraid to mention the subject in their pulpits because they are afraid of losing their jobs. They will preach against homosexuality, adultery, fornication, and pride but the elephant in the room is racism. Jesus died for the church because he loves us all, but we still don't love each other. 2 Chronicles 7:14

Do we really love the truth or have we been conditioned by culture and tradition to accept only what we have been given by our elders? Maybe the division in America is because we're looking through the lens of our own culture. White preachers need to preach the truth about racism, and Black preachers need to preach the truth about personal responsibility. This country is in trouble because preachers are not preaching the whole truth. Black and White ministers should take a long hard look at what we are feeding our congregations. The Church can be no stronger than the truth they receive. John 8:32

Relationships

God has mandated that nature give signs to indicate when a season is over. When the leaves fall, summer is over. When frost covers the ground, fall is over. When flowers bloom, winter is over, and when the temperature rises, spring is over. Farmers who receive abundant harvests have learned to read the signs well. The season is over for some of our relationships and many of us are not reading the signs. If you are always making the calls, giving the cash, making the sacrifices, buying the gifts, and listening to complaints, the season is over. Stop allowing people to weigh you down with their nonsense. Start reading the signs. Ecclesiastes 3:1

A real man wants a woman who will cuddle up in his arms and tell him what she needs. God has placed in men a desire to be appreciated by a woman and when men don't get that they miss something very valuable. No man wants a "strong woman" (strong= non-submissive, self-confident, hard, cold). Any male who depends on his woman to provide for him is a boy not a man. Sister, don't be ashamed to be a woman to your man; it fulfills a need for him. 1 Peter 1-7

Looking for the perfect man or woman? You can stop now. No such person exists. Even if you find one, who's to say that the person will think you are right for him? There is something about everyone at one time or another in their life that you will not like. The bottom line is that relationships take a lot of work. Stop concentrating on the faults of your mate and take a long look in the mirror. It may save your relationship. Philippians 2:3

When a man sees a woman he loves crying, something triggers in him that only he and God can understand. He will gladly die to fix her pain, so the idea of a "strong independent woman" is incomprehensible to a real man. A woman should be strong at being a woman, but godly men are not looking for competition. This is the key to a long biblical, lasting relationship. It is so simple, but many of us are missing it. 1 Peter 3:7

Ladies, we've heard it said that if a man takes care of his mother, he will take care of you. This is true, but it is also true that if his mother takes care of him, he will expect you to take care of him also. It is extremely difficult for a mother to raise her son without the presence of his father because a boy needs that paternal foundation that only a man can give. Many boys have been raised like girls. They expect the world to treat them like they were treated by their mothers. Mom, you have to back away from your sons and let them sink or swim. That's the only way they will mature. Proverbs 4:3

If it walks like a duck, quacks like a duck, and swims like a duck, it's a duck. Believe what people show you and stop making excuses for them. Own the truth that you're being used and move on with your life. You have to face the fact that they have time to do everything else they want to do, but when it comes to you, something always comes up. Stop lying to yourself. Admit that they don't care. It will only hurt once instead of over and over. You can't make an eagle out of a duck. Matthew 7:20

You may have freckles or a mole on your face. Is one of your eyes a little smaller than the other? Are you a little overweight? All of this makes you think that you are unattractive, but nothing can be farther from the truth. If someone loves you, it's the flaws that you hate about yourself which make you unique. Love hides a multitude of faults. If you are with someone who wants you to change to suit them, you are with the wrong person. 1 Peter 4:8

If he left you, you've lost nothing but frustration and headache. If he loved you, he would have attempted to work through the problems you were having and stayed with you. Never chase anything that leaves you on its own freewill and volition. Who chases a snake? Your only recourse now is to pick up the pieces of your life and move on to something greater. Anybody who walks away from you was not yours. You were just holding them until their real love came. Matthew 19:6

I walked into Mom's house and she was sitting in her recliner with the TV off and the remote in her hand. I asked, "Mama why are you sitting here with the television off? I've never come in this house and found the television off." Her response was, "I get tired of seeing the same thing over and over." It makes perfect sense. If you are tired of seeing the same thing over and over in your life, turn off the TV. Are you in a dead-end relationship? An abusive marriage? Surrounded by fake friends? Gambling or drug problem? The remote is in your hand. Romans 12:2

Yes, it hurts when someone cheats on you. Your trust in them is seriously damaged, and your confidence in yourself as a partner for them is compromised. It's really a mess, and you hurt, but it's a bigger mess when you decide to pay them back by cheating on them. Not only do you hurt them by cheating, but you hurt yourself. You may not realize it when you "get even," but your conscience is stretched beyond repair which makes it easier for you to cheat again. I agree. It hurts, but why add hurt on top of hurt? Virtue is its own reward. Let it go or let them go. 2 Peter 1:5

At some point in a relationship you have to stop saying "I love you" and start saying "I love me" because no one deserves verbal/physical abuse, neglect and disrespect. God did not make you to be trampled upon; you're better than that. Stop compromising your integrity and values just to keep someone else happy. Let go. If you don't love yourself, you can't really love anyone else. Love begins with self-respect and then permeates the atmosphere of the lives of others. Charity begins at home and then spreads abroad. 1 Corinthians 13

If a man really wants to see you and doesn't have a car, he will bum a ride. If he doesn't have any money, he will borrow some from his friends. If he doesn't have the time, he will find the time. If he doesn't have a way, he will make a way. Nothing can keep a man from getting to you if he really wants to see you. So why are you spending your money, buying gasoline, driving your car, and interrupting your schedule to go see someone who lies to you? Sometimes what you catch isn't what you want. Proverbs 18:22

When you enter into a relationship under false pretenses, it doesn't last because eventually the real you shows up. Openness is the key to an enduring relationship. Lying about who you are, where you've been and what you have will catch up with you. The most important person to be honest with is you. If the person you're interested in doesn't appreciate the real you, then you're wasting your time. It pays more to be honest than it costs. Keep it real. 1 Timothy 2:2

Religion

Some of us just have too much religion. Keeping all these rules is nerve racking. You shouldn't go to the pulpit without a tie. Dresses must be worn in the sanctuary. You can't wear make-up. There must be a white table cloth must be over the communion table. Music can't be too loud. Preaching is too long. No one can speak in tongues in church. No ministry of Holy Spirit is allowed. Get over it. God moved from your rules to a relationship. Do you have one? Galatians 5:1

There are extremists in all religions, so let's not be too critical. Some extremists fly planes into buildings and some bomb abortion clinics. We need to remember that members of the Ku Klux Klan claimed to be Christians while hanging people from a tree. Interpretation of scripture cannot be done by the natural mind. For proper understanding of the Bible, The Holy Spirit is essential. Whenever a person has an incorrect view of Jesus, they have the propensity to be extreme in their world view. The controversy of all religions will be settled when we see Jesus for who he is. John 14:6

"Some people have just enough religion to make them miserable." ~John Wesley. The pastor stands and makes people feel guilty about their lifestyle while lifting himself and his family as an example of perfection rather than preaching Jesus. As a result, many come and join the church thinking that if they can just be like "them," they will feel better about themselves. There is a church full of pastor followers who have never experienced the joy of forgiveness through Jesus Christ. Consequently, that congregation is esoteric, dull and miserable trying to keep the Ten Commandments. Being a Christian sets you free; it does not put you in a straitjacket. "Where the spirit of the Lord is, there is liberty." 2 Corinthians 3:17

If your religion takes you away from your family and segregates you to only the people in your church, it's not of God. God provides insulation, He does not demand isolation. The true test of religion is not its prescription for holiness but its demonstration of righteousness. We must present ourselves to the world as an example of our faith, and we can't do that locked up in our place of worship. Practice your faith less behind stain glass and more of it in shoe leather. No one can see a light if it stays locked up in a building. Matthew 5:16

Resurrection

Enough with the doom and gloom prophecy. Matthew 24 must be fulfilled, but have you read Revelation 21? There's more waiting for the saints than a hole in the ground. We're not on our way to a funeral but to a feast with our Lord. Don't see the glass half empty. Focus on the victory we have in Jesus.

He died. He was buried. He got up, and he's coming again. This is the story and nothing should be added to it. Preachers, don't be too creative on Sunday. Just tell the story with passion and love. It's not about being prosperous, popular, healthy or super-spiritual. It's all about him. When he died, we died. We are not our own. When he was buried, our sins were buried. When he rose, we arose. We have eternal life. Soon he's coming back to receive his Church. Let's share it. Matthew 28:1

I just learned that nightmares are necessary for brain strength. According to sleep experts, the crazy, sweaty, and horrible dream you had last night actually made your brain stronger. Running down the street naked, drowning in quick sand, even the mummy who cuddled up behind you last night was your friend. It wasn't fun while it was happening. However, after you woke up, it improved memory function, helped you concentrate and relaxed your mind for the day. Some of us are living a nightmare, but if you are a believer, it's only going to make you stronger. The resurrection of Jesus teaches us that we always get up with more power than we had when we got knocked down. Matthew 28:18

Sacrifice

"I'm just here so I won't get fined." This attitude may work for Marshawn Lynch, but it won't work on your job. If you are working on a job, your marriage, or serving in a ministry without commitment to excellence, there will be no promotion. Commitment means making some sacrifices for the present so that rewards will come in the future. Having your cake and eating it too only works in the NFL. Make sacrifices today. It will reap benefits for you tomorrow. Psalms 75:6

Salvation

This Spring I boarded a plane for Washington D.C. to do a revival. As I walked through first class, I saw Lindsey Graham on one side and Jim Clyburn on the other. I thought to myself, "There are three classes of people on this plane—first class, coach, and the crew." As we ascended to 30,000 feet, it hit me. If this plane goes down, there will only be two classes--the saved and the unsaved. It will not matter one day who you are, but it will matter whose you are. Are you saved? Mark 8:36

Selfishness

It's so difficult being me with all the stuff I have to tolerate. If something goes wrong around the house, it has nothing to do with me. If I'm traveling on the interstate and see a horrible crash, it's bad, but it's okay because it wasn't me. When I read the news and see that someone was killed or murdered down the street that is a tragedy. That's what happens in this community. I am thankful it wasn't me. Why are all these homeless people asking for handouts at intersections? They annoy me when I'm enjoying my favorite music on the radio. This could never be me. When I post on Facebook, the ones who don't like my posts must be stupid because they don't like me. What a pitiful world this is that has the audacity to not recognize me. "He who lives for himself has very little to live for." ~Unknown. Matthew 19:19

Self-worth

Trying to impress others is a difficult task. The harder you try to impress them, the more unimpressed they become. Let's stop buying things we don't need, spending money we don't have, trying to impress people we don't even like. God made no mistake when He made us. We are originals not carbon copies. Since God made us unique, let's look in the mirror and enjoy the view. Psalms 139:14

Not every woman is supposed to wear a size eight and not every man is supposed to wear size 32. Our bodies are different. Any doctor will tell this is true. I met a man last week who told me he lost 180lbs just eating right following the dietary laws of the Bible. I wouldn't suggest anyone become a fanatic or just eat kosher, but if you believe that the four food groups are fast, instant, frozen, and chocolate, then you need to rethink your menu. Let's watch what we eat, exercise and rest properly, and stop letting the media, Hollywood and Madison Avenue, make us feel guilty about our God-given sizes and shapes. 1 Corinthians 6:19

Your worth is not determined by someone else's opinion. It doesn't matter what others say or think about you. You are valuable to God. The clothes bought at Walmart and the ones from Neiman Marcus are made from the same fabrics. It's just the label that makes the difference. Toyota and a Bentley will both get you to your destination. Do you have security at the entrance of your housing development? Prisoners do too. It's not what's on the outside that matters but what's on the inside. The outside is temporary, but the inside is forever. We have intrinsic worth because we have a treasure in us that came from God. Believer, you can hold your head up because of who's in you. 2 Corinthians 4:7

Sermons

A bad sermon from a loving heart is far better than a good sermon from an uncaring heart. Many preachers love preaching but don't love the people to whom they are preaching. Enjoying word studies, scriptural research, textual exegesis, and exploring sermon prep-resources for illustrations and examples do not make us good preachers. People don't care how much we know until they know how much we care. Knocking it out of the park on Sunday morning and then walking out the back door without shaking one hand only proves we are preaching for the excitement. Fall in love with people and they will fall in love with your preaching. John 21:15-25

Sharing

God did not mandate isolation as a part of the church's ministry, but He did command separation. In isolation we segregate ourselves totally from the world. In separation there is no participation with the world. There is no holiness in a hole. Winning your family and friends means that you must rub shoulders with them, visit with them, and communicate with them, and laugh with them. If you can't stand cigarette smoke, alcohol, and cussing, you're not ready for prime-time Christianity. Let's stop faking holiness and live it by sharing it with our family and friends. Matthew 5:47

Winos share their bottle. Pot users share joints, and cocaine users share pipes. Why is it that some Christians don't like sharing with one another? The effectiveness of a church is not always what happens after the doxology but what happens after the benediction. How long you hang around after church says a lot about how you enjoy fellow believers. The world needs to see us sharing. Romans 12:13

Sin

God will ultimately use everyone—the saint and the sinner. He uses the saint as an example of what to do and what not to do. We can either wind up like David or Saul. We can become a successful king or an embarrassment to the Kingdom, but either way, we can be used. He uses the sinner to draw us to Himself and to show his power and love for us. The choice is ours. How will God use you? Will you be used as a trophy of grace or disgrace? The choice is ours. Titus 2:11

The pope "let one slip" and everyone was in an uproar. Some people couldn't believe that he actually cursed during a ceremony, but this is a stark reminder that he is human. Never put your spiritual leader on a plateau so high that he can't stay there. We are men and women like everyone else. The fact that he committed a sermonic faux-pas is a testimony of the accuracy of the Bible. Check the record. Abraham lied, Moses murdered, Noah drank, and David played. Let's hang the halos on the hallway hat rack and get about the business of forgiving. Psalms 51:5

Our bodies are wearing down, and besides proper diet and exercise, there is very little we can do about it. When we take synthetic, especially unapproved, chemicals into our bodies, there will be an adverse effect. Have you noticed how there are so many remedies on the market for low testosterone, erectile dysfunction, and failing libido? This stuff is killing people and no one is saying anything in the name of free market. Believers, our bodies are temples. They are designed to wear out because of Adam's sin. Be careful what you put into your body. Ecclesiastes 12:5

I don't have all the answers to the questions in my life, let alone the questions in everyone else's. One thing I'm sure about is the fact that if we don't acknowledge a problem, it will always remain. In order to get the right prescription, there must be a proper diagnosis. The problem in our culture is not that we need reparations for slavery but deliverance from it. It's possible to enslave a body without one's permission, but it takes cooperation to enslave one's mind. The root of slavery is sin that is done willingly, without reservation, and naturally. We must deal with sin first, and Jesus can deliver us from sin! Freedom is not the right to do what you want but the power to do what you ought. Jesus is the true emancipator. John 8:31-41

Some Christians are too Christian to enjoy sinning but too sinful to enjoy Christianity. Some Christians have enough religion to keep them out of the bars and clubs on Saturday night but not enough to take them to mid-week service Wednesday night. Some of us have enough religion to keep us from reading obscene magazines but not enough for us to read our Bibles daily. Why don't we just get all in or all out? Duplicity causes misery. Joshua 24:14-25

Misery: Trying to be, do, or act like something you're not. We can only put on a show for a short time. Sooner or later the curtain has to come down. If you want to be free, come out of the bushes, pull off the fig leaves and tell God the truth. He already knows what you're trying to hide. He's just waiting for you to admit it. The freedom and joy that floods your soul will be overwhelming. 1 John 1:9

The reason some of us are so negative and critical of others is that we are not conscious of the potential of sin in our own heart. Therefore, God has to allow us to fall, so that we will understand that we are capable of the same degradation that we criticize in others. Take notice. Some of the most hard-nosed, insensitive, and judgmental people are always in the news after a scandal. Be careful preaching judgement without compassion because the next casualty may be you. Romans 7:18-25

You will never be tempted to do right. Doing the right thing will often cost you money, time, effort, and pain. Doing wrong is as natural as breathing. The difference is who is leading you. God leads and the devil drives. God will not drive you to do right, but he will lead you in the paths of righteousness. Apologizing is not easy. Turning the cheek is not easy, and refusing to retaliate is not easy, but the rewards are awesome. Let God fight your battle. Be still. Let them hate. God has you covered. Psalms 23

Speech

Let's discipline ourselves today. That is a definite way to protect our memory from remorse, regret and frustration. Once words are deployed, they cannot be retrieved. Colossians 4:6

Words are like missiles. They can be helpful or destructive. It all depends on who controls them. Once released, their effects can last for years. James 3: 1-12

Cursing is the inability to select the right word to express exactly what you want to say. We curse because we think that it will make people know that we are angry, funny, mean or serious. Swearing doesn't make us bad, bold, or bigger; it makes us ignorant. It also reveals what's really in our hearts. The Word declares, "out of the abundance of the heart the mouth speaks." Many kids consider it normal because they have heard it on TV, movies, music and in the home. The world will do what the world does, but it should not be the same in the church. Let's set a standard and watch our mouths. Matthew 12:34

In class the instructor told us never to fire a weapon unless we can see beyond the target. This is not only good advice for shooting a gun but also good advice when using words. The person we're trying to insult, malign, and castigate is not the only one we hurt with our words. Sometimes our children, class, co-workers, or congregations are affected by a mean remark we intended for one person. All of us have influence over someone. Don't abuse that power by "putting someone in their place." There may be some innocent bystanders. Colossians 4:6

"And he said nothing." ~Matthew27:12. Have you ever been in a room with other people or riding in a vehicle and felt a compulsion to talk? We are conditioned from birth to avoid silence. Mama was so happy when we started to talk, and we have been talking ever since. It's hard not to talk especially when we are being accused and persecuted. Let's learn from Jesus and not give a rebuttal to false accusations. It only makes matters worse. People are going to believe what they want, and we can't change their minds by a verbal defense. Say nothing. You know the truth.

Just because a person is articulate doesn't necessarily mean that they are intelligent. Some people can express clearly what they are thinking, but sometimes that's the problem--what they are thinking makes no sense. Others speak slowly, hemming and hawing, but when they have completed their speech, a light bulb goes off in your head. Learn to listen for content rather than excitement and ear candy. 2 Timothy 4:3

It is impossible to defeat an ignorant person in an argument. Why go back and forth with someone who has established their own "alternate truth?" Stop responding to Facebook posts written by ignorant people. You're wasting your time. Education has nothing to do with it. We often confuse a lack of education with being ignorant. Nothing could be farther from the truth. Education only gives an ignorant person the ability to be ignorant intelligently. Having a discussion is an exchange of knowledge, but an argument is an exchange of ignorance. Proverbs 12:15

Spiritual Gifts

Discovering your purpose for being born is as easy as identifying your spiritual gift. God gives us spiritual gifts to perform and complete our purpose. Your gift can be determined by three things:

1. What is it that you can do that comes easy to you but difficult to others?
2. What is the thing that you really enjoy doing for others?
3. What area are most of the compliments you receive in?

It may not necessarily be done in church. Your gift could be in sports, medicine, politics, mechanics, or church. God simply wants you to glorify HIM with your gift, and He will provide your needs as you do it! Wonderful plan, huh? Find your gift and go to work for Him. Proverbs 18:16, Romans12, 1 Corinthians 12, 13, 14

If you want to keep something, give it away. Anything or anyone you hold hostage is never good for you. Let it go. Found a good book? Share it. What about a great opportunity to earn money? Share it. Your spiritual gift is not yours. It belongs to the church. Share it at no charge. God created us to be channels not reservoirs. Keep it moving, and God will give you more. The word "give'" is used 1392 times in the Bible for a reason. Give. Luke 6:38

God created us to be producers not consumers. Any culture, community, or person who consumes and never produces becomes cancerous and inevitably destroys itself. God intends for everything that He made to produce. The sun produces light. Plants produce oxygen. Animals produce carbon dioxide. Soil produces plants, and clouds produce rain. All of God's creation contributes to the existence of life. Every one of us has at least one gift. If you don't use it, you will ultimately lose it. Be liberal in all your deeds, and it will come back to you in some form or another. Proverbs 11:25

The thing that makes us unique can be the source of our deepest agony. What is it that sets you apart from everyone else? Is it your money, talent, athleticism, education, good looks? Be careful that pride doesn't creep into your heart. Whatever comes easy for you and difficult for others is your gift, but don't let your blessing be your downfall. The higher we erect the pedestal for ourselves, the further the distance to a safe landing. Guard your heart with all diligence. 2 Samuel 14:25, 2 Samuel 18:9, 10

Your spiritual gift comes with besetting baggage. If there is no struggle within you, then your ministry will be limited in its impact on the conversion of others. Praise God for your struggle because it's your impetus for changing the lives of people. What an amazing God we serve! He can squeeze His truth through imperfect men and women. 2 Corinthians 12:7

Tattoos

"Do not cut your bodies for the dead or put tattoo marks on yourselves. I am the Lord. ~Leviticus 19:28. I know this verse is taken from the Law and applies to the ancients, but why would God make this mandate for His people? It is because He wants His people to be separate from the people of the land so that all will know that they are set apart for Him. Christianity is not in dress or appearance, but when we devote ourselves to Him; it will show in our appearance.

Testifying

We need to stop testifying about the power of the devil. Every time we talk about how bad we feel, how sick we are, how broke we've been, how our haters are slandering us, how difficult work has become, or how bad our children are, we are giving credence to Satan's ability to make us miserable. Some of us light up a room when we walk out. Stop it. Speak deliverance over your life. Speak victory. Whose report are you going to believe— God or the devil? We're more than conquerors. Greater is he. I can do all things. No weapon formed against us shall prosper. Should I continue? Positive speech will bring positive results. Proverbs 6:2

It's good to be transparent but too much transparency will lessen your impact on people. When giving your testimony, it's not necessary to go into too much detail because most of your listeners don't understand the power of the Gospel to transform. If you are a Christian, you have been delivered from something and God expects you to communicate that to others. Emphasize your new life rather than what you were delivered from. We were responsible for the old. God gets credit for the new, and the latter should be shouted from the roof top. You can tell your story without telling your business. 1 Corinthians 5:17

Testing

God allows some things to happen to us so that other things will happen in us. He, in turn, can do some things through us. If you are a Christian dealing with difficulties, it is because God is preparing you for an assignment. A soldier is tested in boot camp. The doctor is tested in medical school, and Christians are tested in troubles. Be patient in your tribulations, trust the process, and stay faithful. God is at work in you. Philippians 1:12-14

Thankfulness

In 1863 Federal legislation established the fourth Thursday in November as Thanksgiving Day. Thanksgiving is not a day. It should be a way of life. Although people greet each other with, "Happy Thanksgiving," the statement is actually redundant because happiness and thanksgiving go hand and hand. They are inseparable. They are one side of the same coin. It is impossible to have one without the other. Show me someone who is truly happy, and I will show you someone who is truly thankful. On the hand, if you show me someone who is unthankful, I will show you someone who is unhappy. The key to real happiness is to be truly thankful. Ephesians 5:20

If you are not in a thankful mood, take a walk through the halls of hospice care, the hospital or prison. Then turn on the news channel and observe what's happening in Iraq, Afghanistan, Burma and the Philippines. Whatever your problem is today, somebody is a lot worse than you! Just remember that it could be you and you'll feel better about your present condition. Take time to be thankful. 1 Thessalonians 5:18

I've had members of my church say to me, "Pastor, you preach better when you go out to other churches." I thought about that statement and came to the conclusion that it may be because there is a deeper appreciation for my ministry in other places rather than at home. We sometimes become so accustomed to what we have that we fail to appreciate it any longer. This can happen in your marriage, your job, and even with your possessions. Just because you see it every day doesn't necessarily mean that you will see it tomorrow! Show your appreciation to your spouse, children, and friends today and work on your relationships. You might not have them tomorrow.
James 4:13-17

I've stood by a revival evangelist who was greeting and shaking hands with my congregation and heard some of them say to him, "I have never heard that before." My pressure rises because I'm thinking, "If you had been listening rather than sleeping when I said it, you would have heard it." We often make common what we have and get excited about the unfamiliar, but we must stop doing that. Just because you wake up every morning beside your spouse, hear your pastor every Sunday, sit behind your desk every day and call, text and inbox your friends whenever you want, doesn't mean you should take these things for granted. Let's learn to keep life fresh and be thankful for what we have. You can't beat God giving but neither can you beat Him taking away. Job 1:20-22

Enjoying the blessings of God without thankfulness is demonic. Psalms 100:4

You can't enjoy the stars without the night,
You can't experience victory without a fight,
You'll never appreciate medicine without pain,
You can't enjoy sunshine without rain.

Life hurts sometimes, but it was designed that way. God is teaching us all to be thankful for His blessings. Offer to Him an "in spite of praise." Habakkuk 3:17-19

Some people came from nothing, so they appreciate everything. Others came from everything, so they appreciate nothing. There's something inherently good about hard work that makes us appreciate what we've attained. Parents, you do your children a disservice by giving them handouts. Why not give them a hand up by giving them assignments, chores, around the house. They will thank you later. Ecclesiastes 10:18

Trusting God

We like to praise God when He opens a door but cry when He closes one. We tend to thank God more for the things He does but overlook the things He doesn't do. The same God who delivers sometimes, for His own reasons, doesn't deliver. We must learn that God is God and we have to trust His judgment and thank and praise Him. Can you imagine what our lives would be like if God answered all our prayers? Aren't you glad that you're not in charge of your life? Relax. Let your requests be known to God but let Him have the final decision. Revelation 3:7

"Every day with Jesus gets sweeter and sweeter." is a saying we've picked up over the years, but it is not necessarily true. Sometimes a sour day is followed by one a lot worse and a darker day might proceed a dark day. Still, you can't determine your walk with the Lord until all your days are counted. When all our days have been counted, we will understand that it is better to have walked with Jesus than to spend our lives for the world, the flesh and the devil. If you're sad, sick or troubled today, don't put God on your schedule, just hold on a little while longer, He knows and wants the best for you. Jeremiah 29:11

Trusting God is not enough. If you are on a railroad track and the train is approaching, you don't just sit there and say "I'm trusting God." If you don't get out of the way, you're dead. Many of us sing, "I'm standing on the promises," but we are actually sitting on the premises. You should actually do as much as possible. Take your medicine, prepare yourself for the position, study your lesson, work on the situation with all your might, get a job and then trust God. Man's extremities are God's opportunities. Matthew 4:1-11

"Being blessed" doesn't necessarily mean carefree, prosperous, and healthy. Sometimes God will bless us with suffering. If pain will draw us closer to God, He will sometimes allow it. If you're suffering, it does not mean that God has forsaken you. It may be because God is developing you for an assignment. Only He knows His plan for us, so trust His heart when you can't see His hand. 2 Corinthians 12:8-10

For the sake of argument, let's just say you had complete control of this world. What would you do? What decisions would you make concerning the Middle East? Who would you let live and who would you let die? How would you go about deciding the destiny of the seven billion people in the world? The truth is you wouldn't even know where to start. We must learn that we can't dictate our own destiny, let alone anyone else's. This world is in God's hand and we must accept

His plans and simply trust Him. Give up being CEO of the universe and trust God. It's liberating. Colossians 1:16, 17

An anchor's weight slows the boat down and the sailors are really unaware that it's even on board. The crew sees its presence as common practice for mariners; therefore, many of them never know its value. When the storm comes, everyone is thankful that it's on the ship. We would never know the value of Christ if there were no storms in our lives. God sends storms in our lives so that we can value the anchor. The very storm that rocks the boat also moves it. Hebrews 6:17-19

It doesn't matter what they think or what they said, what matters is what you think and how you respond. Encourage yourself in the Lord. Get by yourself. Get in your car, closet, bathroom, or storage room, and talk to the Lord about it. Once you've finished, leave it in His hands. He's going to work it out! Believe this! Jeremiah 33:3

A God that can be predicted and understood is not worthy of our worship. We don't know why a mother was killed on the highway while her baby was spared in the back seat. We don't know why a preacher died in a fiery plane crash. We will never understand why devout Christians die early and drug dealers live to be ripe old age. This world is in God's hands and we must trust Him. Our God is mysterious and His ways are far beyond our comprehension. It is tragic when we interpret tragedy. Sit back, relax, and let God do the driving. Isaiah 55:8, 9

"God can take a crooked stick and hit a straight lick." ~ A. L. Patterson. Your situation may be overwhelming and appear impossible to solve, but Anything + God's hands = possibility. God will do one of two things with your impossibility; He will fix the situation or fix you for the situation. Put it in His hands. Matthew 19:26

161

My old truck wouldn't start, so I called a friend to give me a jump. He hooked up the cables—one red, one black, and immediately my truck started. The red was positive, the black was negative, but it took both to start my truck. It takes both positive things and negative things to generate power. Too much positive is never good, and neither is too much negative. Whenever there is a changing of the guard in Washington D.C., many of us are feel melancholy, but God knows what we need. Trust Him. Believe it or not, if you are saved, the change will ultimately empower you. Philippians 4:12-13

Once we get our theology packaged, neatly wrapped with a bow, and safely stowed away on a shelf, God comes along and knocks it to the floor. When I was in my thirties, I thought I knew why people suffered and why hurricanes and tornadoes went through certain cities and bypassed others. I could explain scripturally why some people got cancer and others did not. I knew why third world countries had poverty and America enjoyed prosperity. The older I got, the less I knew about life and this world. Today, my only advice to anyone going through trouble is to trust God. He has never failed me or anyone who trusted Him. Even when we can't see our way, he's at work. Isaiah 55:8, 9

Truth

The truth will set you free only if you believe the truth. John 8:31-32

Truth will always prevail. If you have ever been lied on, you know how it hurts. "Sticks and stones will break my bones but words won't hurt me" is not an accurate statement. Words do hurt. The difference between a lie and the truth is the difference between lighting and thunder. Lightning travels faster than thunder, but the lightening gets more attention. So it is with a lie. Never attempt to "straighten out a lie." Just be patient; time is on your side. Proverbs 6:16-19

"God can do anything He wants to do." Wrong. There is one thing that God can't do. No matter how you pray and fast, praise and worship, or sacrifice and honor His name. The one thing God can't do is change His Word. When you lose a loved one, go through sickness and suffer with trials and tribulations, God cries with you, but He has to allow it because He said in His Word to Adam that it would happen. Therefore, we have comfort in knowing that He is a God of absolute truth. When you pray, you don't have to beg or shout. Simply remind Him of His Word. Numbers 23:19

Truth has been sacrificed on the altar of popularity in many pulpits in America. No one who preaches the truth will ever be popular in the eyes of the world because they hate the truth. When a doctor tells them they need more tests, they take the tests. If Uncle Sam says taxes have been raised, they pay them, but if they hear the truth, they kill the messenger. One of the ways you will know a true believer is that they love the truth especially when it applies to them. A true prophet doesn't expect to be given the key to the city but forced out of it. John 15:18-27

If you always tell the truth, you won't have to remember what you said. "A lie has to be propped up." ~Squire Williams. What's more dangerous-- a clock five minutes wrong or one five hours wrong? A clock five minutes wrong is more dangerous because it's closer to the truth. Satan mixes truth with error to deceive. In fact, a half-truth is a whole lie. Tell the truth even when it hurts your image. John 14:6

Victory

Jesus never wrote a book. He never painted a picture. He never composed a poem or a song. He never traveled more than 50 miles from his birthplace. He didn't have a formal education. He never raised an army. He never owned property, but yet he changed history forever because he had purpose. When a person is following purpose,

163

never count them out of the fight. We don't need this world's resources to be great. 1+God=Victory. Philippians 4:13.

Vision

Before Michelangelo began the statue of David, he envisioned what he thought David would look like. Then he took a chunk of marble and removed everything that didn't look like his vision. When he finished, he had a celebrated masterpiece that's been duplicated around the world. God has a vision for each of us. He removes little by little that which doesn't look like His vision. Sometimes it's not an enjoyable process, but when He's through with us, we will be trophies of His grace. Jeremiah 29:11

We will become tomorrow what we envision today. Helen Keller (who was blind) once said, "There's a worse thing than being born blind, that's being born with sight and no vision." Let's start thinking today like what we want to be tomorrow. Want to lose weight? Start exercising today. Want to be wealthy? Start developing a plan today. Want a successful home? Start chastising your children today. Nothing happens positively to us unless we can see it in our minds first. We are becoming what we see. Habakkuk 2:2

Walt Disney was told, "No one wants to see a cartoon of a mouse!" The Wright Brothers were told, "If man was meant to fly he'd have wings!" Jesus was told, "You're of the devil!" If you have a plan A, also develop a plan B to accomplish your goals because you will get opposition. If plan A fails, you can rely on plan B or C. Even a rat knows this. Whenever you see one hole in the wall, rest assured there's a second hole somewhere because that rat knows that the cat may be waiting at the first. You plan to fail when you fail to plan. Get a vision for your life. Ecclesiastes 11:1-6

If someone throws a knife at you there are only two ways to catch it. It has to be caught by the blade or by the handle. If you catch it by the blade, you will bleed. If you catch it by the handle, you're in control. Anyone with vision, a plan, and a purpose becomes a target. The truth is that's good news because the darts thrown in your direction become weapons to use against your enemy. Spend no time tracking down lies people told on you but focus on your God-given purpose as a believer. It is choice not chance that determines your destiny. You were created to win. Romans 12:19-21

Wisdom

Information is at our finger tips. We can Google and instantly find an answer about anything we want to know. The problem today is not information but how to use that information to solve this world's ills. Information comes from looking around but wisdom comes from looking up. Wisdom only comes from listening to God and applying what you heard. We have college degrees, but not enough sense to say, "Good Morning" to each other. Information has made our world a neighborhood, but we are still filled with hate, racism and bigotry. We can travel from one continent to another in a matter of minutes, but when we arrive, we still may not have peace in our hearts. Church, we must pray for wisdom. James 1:5

Witness

There's a difference between goat and sheep, wheat and thorns, light and darkness, righteousness and unrighteousness. These are terms the Bible uses to describe the difference between the Church and the world. We nullify that difference when we act, dress, and talk like the people we're trying to bring to Christ for the sake of fitting in." If we are going to be like the world, why should they even consider becoming like us? Don't be ashamed to be different. It was the Holy Spirit that made you different to make you a witness.
2 Corinthians 6:17

Some of us go to church as witnesses and some go as the jury. The difference, of course, is that witnesses testify what they have seen and heard, but the jury has to be convinced. A good memory will help your worship experience. If you have been delivered and the joy of the Lord permeates your soul, no one should have to convince you that the Lord is worthy of your worship. Let's go to church Sunday as witnesses rather than the jury. He's good all the time. Psalms 100:4

Women

Act like a woman and think like a man? Why not act like a woman and think like God? Sisters, be careful with some of the literature on the shelves because most of the stuff out there is not biblically based. Your mind is your most prized possession because it includes your soul. The same word in the Greek language is often used for both which means your mind and soul are interchangeable. The Bible instructs, "Let this mind be in you which was also in Christ Jesus." Philippians 2:5. Want to get and keep your man? Live for Jesus. If your man leaves you, let him go because he wasn't yours in the beginning.

To all the experts on women just stop it. Tyler Perry, Dr. Phil and Steve Harvey all have advice for women. Where did they take Women 101? The truth is no one will ever know women. Men should get to know themselves. God created women to be responsive to their man which means women will act in accordance to how she is treated. If she's loved and cherished, she acts in kind. If she's neglected and misused, you've never had a stronger opponent. The problem is the heart of the man. When a man gets his heart right with God, then and only then will his woman act accordingly. Save the trip to the bookstore to read the next genius on women and get down on your knees and find yourself. 1 Corinthians 11:8, 9

Work

There is no such thing as a demeaning job. If you earn a living honestly, never be ashamed of what you do. Anyone who makes a living from ill-gotten gain will never enjoy it. God has promised it. Proverbs 10:2-3. If you sweep floors, drive a truck, or mow lawns for a living, you are happier than a person who flies in his own personal jet from city to city, lying to the public, trying to win the Oval Office. Happiness will never be found in dishonesty. Ezekiel 22:13

There is no such thing as a lousy job. If you are working for a living each day, thank God for the health and strength to perform the work and for the job. An honest day's work for honest pay is a blessing from God. Do your job with excellence and appreciation and sooner or later someone else will recognize your worth. Then a promotion will be in your future. Your today will not define your tomorrow. Promotion comes from sacrificing not complaining. Psalms 75:6, 7

Worrying

"So don't worry about tomorrow, for tomorrow will bring its own worries. Today's trouble is enough for today." Matthew 6:34. Isn't it amazing that God supplies us with troubles? Why would He do such a thing? It is simple. He wants us to trust Him, depend on Him and converse with Him daily! Did you ever think that the problem you have could have been given to you to keep you on your knees? God delights in fellowship with us so much that He suffers us to have troubles each day. Yet, in the midst of them He promises, "I will be with you."

Ninety percent of what we worry about never comes to pass. We can do nothing about the five percent of it that does, and usually the other five percent that does come to pass is not as bad as we predicted.

So why do you worry? God is in control. Relax, chill, and enjoy the ride. Matthew 6:33

"The path of least resistance is what makes both rivers and men crooked" ~ Unknown. God has provided some troubles for us so that we will keep seeking Him. At what times did you learn the most about yourself and God? It was when trouble came in your life. Today is the tomorrow that you worried about yesterday, so what good did it do? Worrying is like a rocking chair. It gives you something to do, but it gets you nowhere. Since through faith all things are possible, then the greatest problem we have believes what God says. Trust God's timing. Matthew 6:33-34

There is no emergency in heaven. God is not pacing the floor and biting His nails trying to figure out what to do about what's happening on planet Earth. He is not assembling a planning committee nor is He assessing damage control measures and putting in place Homeland Security agencies to assist catastrophic victims. Relax and stop fretting over what's going on in Washington, DC. God is in control. Psalms 37

God can take a seed and dirt and give us the mighty oak. He can take his breath and dust and give us life. He can take hydrogen and oxygen and give us water. He can take the past, the present, and the future and give us time. He can take His Son and put him on a Cross and give us eternal life. Tell me again why are you worried about your little problem? Matthew 19:26

Worship

"I don't like that Church. I don't like his preaching. I'm looking for a Church that I can enjoy. I don't like that song. I can't stand to hear them sing, and that church is too noisy." Heard any of these statements lately? Have you made any of them? Have you ever considered that it's not about you? We should go to worship with pleasing God as our focus not fulfilling our own desires for "enjoying the service." We should never go to church to enjoy ourselves, but to make sure the Lord has a blast. The only way to do that is to worship Him. Let's pledge to stop looking around in church investigating others and look up to God in adoration. Psalms 121:1

What's more important having blessings or the one who blesses? Having creation or the Creator? Having stuff or the Savior? It just seems that the pulpit has gone awry in placing more emphasis on what God can do and give rather than God Himself. How would you feel if one of your children kept running to you wanting expensive things and then never visited you, never wanted to be in your presence, and got mad when you stopped handing out freebies? Well, God wants us to worship Him for who He is not for what He gives. All this materialistic preaching will pass away but God's Word will stand forever. Revelations 4:1

I noticed something about "The Voice." Every contestant walks up to the microphone with one thing on their mind—to impress the judge. They didn't care what other contestants think. They are not interested in the genre of music the other participants sing. They don't even look in the direction of others. Their focus is on the judges. What if we all went to church like that? What if we made our focus impressing the Judge? Most people show up at church to judge rather than to impress the Judge. "I don't like contemporary music. I don't like traditional hymn. I can't stand those ole fogy worship services." Has it ever dawned on you that worship is not for you? It's for the Judge. At the end of the day all that will matter is what the Judge thinks. Revelations 22:9

There are times when you don't want to turn to your neighbor, slap somebody high-five, or go tell three people. Sometimes you simply want to bask in the glory of His presence and worship Him in silence and awe. Exciting worship doesn't always put on an emotional display. It's often pensive and reflective. Don't be mad if I don't jump when you tell me to. It's not you I came to see. 1 Kings 19:12

Worship is not easy. It's not fun, nor is it cheap. Real worship costs. Many of us don't receive anything from a worship experience because we go to enjoy ourselves. We should never go to church to enjoy ourselves but to make sure God enjoys Himself. To worship we must focus our attention away from ourselves and put it on God. We must avoid distractions, risk being labeled sanctimonious, and bring God a sacrificial gift. None of this is easy, fun or cheap. When we engage in biblical worship, only then does the satisfaction and enjoyment come and fill our souls. Genesis 22:2

Youth

The term "conservative evangelical" is an oxymoron. Conservative means "holding to traditional values and cautious about change." The church will never be effective today unless it changes its strategies to reach the millennials who will run the world in ten years. The biggest liberal in the history of the church was Jesus Christ. He challenged the status quo about the Law of Moses, the concept of worship practices of the Jews in the synagogue, and Jewish resistance to the political establishment, just to name a few. No one can be conservative and evangelical at the same time. The church should be concerned about the souls of humanity not espousing a political agenda that caters to the wealthy.

Listen before you lecture so you will know what to say in your lecture. Let's pay attention to our kids and grandkids because they can teach us something. Nothing turns off millennials more than an older person standing on a soapbox barking out advice. Sure, we have the responsibility to guide our young people in the right direction, but we must first gain their confidence. To do this, we must respect them by listening to them. Young people have opinions too. 1 Timothy 4:12

Just because it's exciting, exhilarating and even inspirational doesn't mean that God is in it. Young people need to be taught that emotional upheaval has nothing to do with God. Worship means being broken before God to the point that nothing else matters in this world but God. This is the reason many Christians have to go through much pain and suffering. God wants us to see Him. Bodily exercise profits little, but worship is eternal. 1 Timothy 4:8

Not all young people are trifling and lazy. I usually hear a soft female voice in hotels announcing, "Housekeeping." One day I heard a voice with bass in it. When I opened the door, he said, "Do you need service this morning?" I said, "No bruh, I'm cool." He responded, "Thanks man. Now I can leave earlier so I can go to my other job." This young guy is working two jobs to support his family. We often make unfair generalizations of people because of age, race, gender, and religion. Get to know a person before you make an assessment of them.

Never be mad at the overzealous young Christians who are just happy to be a part of the Kingdom. Be sad for the unpassionate, laid back, unexcited believers who think that God owes them something. The church has survived Egyptian bondage, the Babylonian Captivity, the Persian Invasion, and Roman Suppression because of passionate believers. The Bible never uses the word overzealous; it only forbids zeal without knowledge. Lukewarm Christians are doing more harm to the cause of Christ than our overzealous youth. Stop criticizing zeal and condemn lackadaisicalness. Revelation 3:16

99143107R00101

Made in the USA
Lexington, KY
13 September 2018